JESUS BEN JOSEPH

An Introduction to
Jesus the Jew

JESUS BEN JOSEPH

An Introduction to
Jesus the Jew

Walter Riggans

MARC
OLIVE PRESS

First published 1993

ISBN 1 85424 227 X (Monarch)
ISBN 0 904054 16 0 (Olive Press)

Unless otherwise indicated, biblical quotations are from the
Revised English Version

British Library Cataloguing in Publication Data
A catalogue record for this book is available from
the British Library.

Production and Printing in England for
MONARCH PUBLICATIONS
PO Box 163, Tunbridge Wells TN3 0NZ
by Nuprint Ltd, Harpenden, Herts AL5 4SE

CONTENTS

ACKNOWLEDGEMENTS

I would like to acknowledge the graciousness of Dr David Stern in allowing me to quote extensively from his *Jewish New Testament* in chapter 8. His commitment to introducing both Jewish and Christian people to the Jewishness of Jesus has been a great inspiration to many of us. All the other biblical quotations are taken from the Revised English Bible.

My thanks also go to the editor of the Journal, *Themelios,* for allowing me to use the material which formed the basis for an article in that Journal in 1992.

Finally, I would also like to acknowledge the graciousness of my family, who, as usual, bore much of the brunt of the cost of the time needed to write this book.

FOREWORD

It is very difficult to see inside someone else's imagination, but I have always had the feeling that when I read the narratives of the life of Jesus, they do not mean for me what they mean for my non-Jewish friends. We come from such different starting points. I read about the Feast of Tabernacles, the Feast of the Dedication, the Sabbath, and other familiar Jewish events and I automatically place Jesus within the context of the festivals, traditions and culture I knew so well as I grew up. Although contemporary Judaism has undergone a certain metamorphosis since the days when Christ walked the earth, much is the same.

So I am very glad that Walter Riggans has taken the time to put Jesus back into his 'kosher' setting. It does make a difference. It throws a totally different complexion on so many of the gospel stories. It explains many of the things Jesus did, illuminates what he said, highlights the radical nature of his message. It also brings Jesus, the man, alive, which makes Jesus, the Son of God, more accessible. For we find someone who was warm, vibrant, funny, courageous and stimulating, fully part of the world in which he was raised, yet apart enough to see and challenge its foibles. The world never changes. And Jesus, the Jew, compels each of us to take a closer look at many of our own religious preconceptions.

Michele Guinness

1

The Fascination Of Jesus Ben Joseph

I wonder how many books and articles have been written about Jesus? Most of the words will have come from people who worship him as the Son of God, but of course a lot has been written by people who are either antagonistic to the Christian faith or merely fascinated by the enigma of Jesus. *And* all of these books and articles—not to mention the sermons and lectures—have been produced in, or translated into, many different languages.

Jesus has not been neatly put into a pigeon-hole even yet!

Each new generation discovers him for itself, and wrestles with the implications of his life and teaching. I am one of those people who grew up without giving him too much thought until my late teens, when I discovered that he was the most wonderful person I had ever met. After my own period of wrestling with this fact I became a Christian, which is to say that I came to realise and acknowledge that Jesus really is the Son of God, and not simply a great person.

In my case, the encounter with Jesus in the first place came about in the context of meeting a group of people who were already Christians. All of them were, like myself, non-Jews who lived in Scotland. In a short space of time I met Christians from all over the world. But it was to be a long time before I met, or even heard of, *Jewish* people who believed that Jesus was the Messiah of Israel and the Son of God.

Since that time, I have met thousands of such Jewish people. On the other hand I have met even more Jewish people who not only reject all talk of Jesus being the Messiah, but who also despise any Jewish person who believes that he is the Messiah. And yet, one way or another, there can be no doubt whatsoever that Jesus is more of a source of fascination for Jewish people today than he has been for some time. In this book I hope to help Jewish people with an interest in Jesus to come some way to meeting him for themselves. He is the most extraordinary person imaginable: full of inner strength, deep peace, and a joy which transforms life.

However. The Jewish community as a whole resists any attempt to present Jesus in a favourable light to Jewish people. Before we proceed to look at some of the reasons why it is impossible to understand Jesus if we separate him from his Jewish nature and life-setting, it will be useful to note something of the Jewish (and Christian, in certain cases) antagonism to a Jewish Jesus.

2

Antagonism To A Jewish Jesus

'If Jesus really was Jewish, then how come Jewish people don't accept him as Jewish?' This is one of the commonest questions asked when Christians try to persuade people of the fact that Jesus was very much a faithful and devout Jewish man of his time and place. And of course it is a perfectly reasonable question to ask. Wouldn't you expect Jewish people to be the best judges of what it is to be Jewish? In a book about circumcision, Passover, and the like, you would focus on the teachings of Jewish people.

In a book about the divinity of Christ, or the Christian doctrine of the Trinity, etc., you would devote most of your attention to the teachings of the Church and Christian theologians. Most people seem happy to keep things like this, which is to say in neat boxes, leaving people to believe what they want, so long as it doesn't interfere with the lives of others.

In this spirit, most Rabbis today would be happy

for the Church to believe what it likes about its own doctrines and creeds concerning Christ. But it is quite a different matter when you say that Jesus of Nazareth, or to give him his Jewish name, Jesus ben Joseph, was *Jewish*. To claim that the founder of Christianity and the head of the Church was Jewish is to come out of the box and cross over the boundary which some have spent a lot of time and effort creating. What right does the Church have to make that claim, especially in the light of the wholesale antagonism which has characterised Jewish-Christian relations down the centuries?

There is a lot of antagonism among both Jews and Christians to such a claim about Jesus being Jewish. Here is part of a typical conversation:

> 'I've been enjoying our chats about the different outlooks of Judaism and Christianity, and it's certainly been an eye-opener for me to see the way you read your Bible. But I do think you have the wrong end of the stick in some of your ideas about Jesus and how we read the gospels. Could I give you a copy of one of the gospels to read for yourself?'

> 'No, I'm sorry, but I can't do that. I know that you mean well, and that you are not like other Christians in your attitude to Jewish people, but you don't represent the Church. You're the exception which proves the rule. Jesus has been nothing but trouble to my people from the very beginning. He called us hypocrites and legalists; he wanted an end to our religion; he taught his disciples that he had come to bring a sword to the

Jewish world, not peace; and he believed that he— a simple carpenter if we are to believe the story— had become divine. And from that time on, the Church has done its best to see to it that Jesus and Jews are kept on opposite sides of the fence. You're either Jewish or you believe in Jesus.'

'But don't you believe that Jesus himself was Jewish?'

'No, the Rabbis are right. He was maybe Jewish by an accident of birth, but his life and teachings were not at all Jewish. Look, Karl Marx was Jewish too, but look at the mess Marxism made of life for Jews and everybody else in Communist countries. Marx was an atheist for goodness sake! If Jesus' mother was Jewish—even if he was illegitimate—then he would have Jewish blood in him, but that doesn't make him a real Jewish person, let alone a religious leader worth listening to.'

Here is the first issue, then. It is not surprising that Jewish people do not appreciate the Jewishness of Jesus given their terrible treatment at the hands of Christians throughout the generations. Christians stress time and again how radically *different* the Christian faith is from Judaism; they speak as if freedom and grace and love only came into the world when Jesus was born; as if Judaism has no real knowledge of God within it; as if Jewish traditions and festivals, Jewish ways of reading the Bible, and Jewish attitudes to life and law are not only deficient but actually contrary to the will of God. The ultimate dismissal of the Jewish experience is, of course, the traditional Christian teaching that God has in fact rejected the Jewish people and replaced them in his affection and purposes with the Church.

What is more, this Church of God has been fundamentally opposed to the survival of any Jewishness within it. Focusing again on our central question as to whether it makes sense to call Jesus Jewish or not, one of the most telling points for the Jewish community has been the treatment of Jewish people who have either been coerced or manipulated into professing faith in Christ, being baptised and joining the Church, or who may even have joined the Church for what seem to be genuine motives. What has the Church done in the name of its founder, Jesus? It has insisted that any such Jewish person not only formally renounce his/her Jewish religion, but also renounce her/his Jewishness altogether. All traces of Hebrew or Jewish culture must be jettisoned, and the new 'Christian' must live, worship, and relate like the Gentiles whose church he/she has now joined.

The story is often told of a Jewish person in America in the 1960s who came to a real faith in Jesus as Israel's Messiah, and who subsequently approached a local church with a view to becoming a member. All went well until the morning service when he was to say something about his spiritual pilgrimage to the congregation before formally being accepted as a member. After he had spoken, and with no prior notice at all, the pastor produced a ham sandwich and asked the new Jewish believer to eat it there and then as a proof that he was no longer under the bondage of Judaism! This kind of thing makes a sensitive and mature Christian cringe with shame.

True stories could also be told about Jewish believers who have been forbidden by the church leaders in their congregations to circumcise their sons, or to give their children Hebrew names, or to celebrate Passover in any way, shape, or form.

If a Jew who believes in Jesus isn't allowed to be Jewish, then what reason is there for Jewish people to believe that Jesus himself was Jewish, let alone to consider that this should be an important fact? And so for centuries now the Jewish community's leaders have forbidden their people to even read a gospel, far less reflect on the person, Jesus. His Jewishness has been lost to the Jewish people.

The prejudice of the churches against the Jewish people has led to a Jewish prejudice against Jesus.

Prejudice is a terrible thing no matter where you find it. It is often based, of course, on nothing more than an ignorant fear of something which is unknown, or strange. Sometimes it is based on one particular bad experience or feeling which is then blown up and generalised for the whole of life. But then again there are cases of prejudice where one people's experiences at the hands of another have been so consistently awful, that it would be quite surprising if that people did *not* pre-judge the other to be not worthy of trust or friendship.

Such is the case with the Jewish people's prejudice against the Jew, Jesus.

Or it would be the case, except that the Jewish people have had no such bad experiences at the hands of Jesus. Their reaction is based, rationally enough, some would say, on their awful experiences at the hands of Christians down through the centuries. All those generations of antisemitism have convinced the Jewish community that there can be nothing of positive value for them in the life of Jesus.

But let's look now for a moment at the Christian world and its response to the claim that Jesus was Jewish. Here is a fragment from a typical conversation:

'I don't understand you. You're talking as if Jesus was an Anglican! And an English Anglican at that!'

'Well what about you? To hear you talk sometimes, I'm not sure you even think Jesus was a Christian!'

'Actually I don't think he was a Christian. What I mean is that he was a Jew, worshipping in a synagogue, reading the Bible in Hebrew, living a Jewish life under the Roman oppression in Galilee. He didn't belong to a church; he didn't recite Christian creeds; he didn't look like me or you, he looked like a Middle Eastern Jew! I know that he's my Saviour, and I believe that with all my heart, but I also want to know what his life on earth was like. What kind of a person was he? Did he stick out like a sore thumb, or were there sides to him that seemed to fit in easily with his society? And when you want to meet him in that way you can't avoid the fact that he was a Jew from Galilee at the time of Herod!'

'Well I don't think he fitted in at all. Just like today. He's not like anybody else at all. He's totally different in the way he thinks, the way he acts, the way he teaches, the things that he really teaches about, and everything. Sure he was born in Bethlehem, and all that, but for goodness sake he

had to be born somewhere! That's not really important.
When you look at the Jewish religion at that time you can see that it was dead and useless. Jesus was a totally new start and had nothing in common with the other religious people around him at the time.

Being Jewish was an accident of birth, really. The important thing is to be a new creation in Christ, and Jesus came to make this possible for everybody. Being Jewish isn't important—Jesus is way beyond all that. Besides, if you start telling people that Jesus was Jewish then they'll get the wrong impression altogether. Christianity is about freedom from legalism, and freedom from dry religion. Jews are too powerful as it is, without making them feel as if they own Jesus too.'

Here is the second issue that we have to face. A surprisingly large percentage of Christians have not only never thought of Jesus as Jewish, but they react antagonistically when people try to point out that he was. It's often even worse if someone tries to convince them that it is important that we know that Jesus was Jewish.

There are two reasons for this which constantly surface. First of all there is the awful fact of antisemitism, which is still as real as ever, and which is present in Christian communities just as it is in the wider world. And so Christians who share this antisemitism, even at subtle levels, and who therefore want to distance themselves from the Jewish people and Jewish perspectives on life, will either deny

Jesus' Jewishness, or at least reject any significance in the fact that Jesus was Jewish.

The other reason that Christians give for marginalising the Jewishness of Jesus is their sincere conviction that Jesus the man was so fundamentally distinct from any and all other people that we simply cannot class him alongside the rest of humanity in any meaningful way. Therefore his Jewishness, which is taken to be just another side of his humanness, is seen as irrelevant to any search for significant insights into who Jesus was, or into his impact on the society around him.

Both of these Christian reluctances to recognise that Jesus was a Jew of his time and place are based, in their different ways, on the desire to distance Jesus from his Jewish world. It can come as a real shock to Christians to realise the significance of the fact that Jesus was Jewish!

What do we find then as we look around our churches and our synagogues today? We find that both Jews and Christians, for their own reasons, express caution at best, and hostility at worst, when asked to consider that Jesus cannot be fully understood and appreciated until we take his Jewish roots and his Jewish life seriously. This book is an attempt to help both Jews and Christians come to realise nonetheless that this is a vital step for them to be able to take. My particular concern, however, is that Jewish people be given the necessary confidence to study the life and teaching of Jesus for themselves.

Of course there are now a good number of books available on this subject. And many of the best of these have been written by Jewish scholars! My task is to communicate some of this scholarship to the wider Jewish and Christian public. In particular, I am concerned about the sensitivities of Jewish people who are the products of a culture which has taught them that it is disloyal to the Jewish community to read a gospel or think seriously about Jesus. I have met very many Jewish people who are afraid that it will be a religious outrage if they consider that Jesus was not an outsider but a worthy teacher and guide.

Here is a little bit of another recent conversation:

> 'I don't know what to do here. I feel I owe it to myself to read one of the gospels to see what I make of Jesus. But I also feel guilty about it at the same time.'

> 'I don't understand. Why should you feel guilty?'

> 'Because my family would tell me that I owe it to them not to have anything to do with Jesus or the New Testament. Lots of Jews in the past refused to give in to the bullying of the Church and get baptised. They were really prepared to be martyred rather than join the Church and study the gospels. And here am I casually deciding to pick one up and read it. It would hurt them a lot.'

Many Christians reading this will simply not understand the issue which faces Jewish people in this situation. But it is a real one, and it must be respected. The last thing which I would wish would be that any Jewish person felt pressurised into reading a gospel or talking about Jesus.

There is no doubt that Christians need to learn more about the Hebrew Bible (usually called the Old Testament by Christians).

Nor can there be any doubt that they need to learn about the living faith of Judaism, and about the significant figures who have made Judaism what it is today (in all its different forms).

Indeed this will all help them to appreciate why Jewish people feel the way they do about all things Christian. It seems that the bulk of the work being done by the many Jewish-Christian dialogue groups today lies in this very area. And this will certainly help Christians to develop the sensitivity which they need in building meaningful relationships with Jewish people.

But on the other hand it is surely also true that Jewish people need to learn more about the New Testament, and particularly about Jesus himself. It will come as a great surprise to many Jewish people to realise how much important research about Jesus is being done by Jewish scholars. He is no longer taboo.

Christians, for their part, need to reflect more deeply on the humanness of Jesus. At the heart of the Christian faith is our set of beliefs about the person and work of Christ. But the word 'Christ' is nothing more than a translation, via Greek, of the Hebrew word 'Messiah'. At the heart of our faith, then, is our belief in Jesus, the Messiah. At the heart of our teaching about the Messiah is the wonder of the incarnation, by which we mean that God took on human nature and came to live among us on earth.

Perhaps it would be helpful at this point to stress that Christians do not believe that Jesus was a man who somehow became a god.

This sort of thing is often heard when someone wants to take potshots at the Christian faith. The teaching of the incarnation is that God became human, not the other way round. This does not make it less of a miracle, of course, but it is a case of a real miracle, rather than a form of idolatry in which people worship a man.

Nor is it a mere accident of history that the incarnate Son of God became a *Jewish* man in the land known by the Romans as Palestine. Only the Jewish people had been given promises of the coming of this Messiah; only they were expecting him and praying for his coming; and only they had lived as the covenant people of God over the generations.

If Jesus had been born at another time, in another place, and as part of another people, then he would not at all be the Jesus whom we know and love from the gospels! His Jewishness was part of him; it deeply influenced him; it helped to define him. And let us not forget that it defined the disciples and everyone else around him. So we move on in this short book to examine something of the modern re-discovery of Jesus the Jew. Jews and Christians alike have nothing to lose from getting to know him better, and both will feel the benefit of letting him speak for himself out of the context of the gospels.

Let us then move on with one of the most startling statements to have been made by a leading Jewish

23

figure in our century. Martin Buber, a German Jewish philosopher and theologian, and a seminal Zionist thinker of his generation (1878-1965), whose name ranks among the giants of our day for his insights into personal relationships, was fascinated by the person of Jesus. Buber was fully committed to the cause of Jewish survival in the modern world,and a large part of his work lay in the area of Jewish-Christian dialogue. He actually wrote the following in his book, *Two Types of Faith*, in which he compared what he saw as the typical, and different, insights and world views of Judaism and Christianity:

> From my youth onwards I have found in Jesus my great brother.[1]

To be sure, this did not mean that Buber had 'become a Christian' or the like. But on the other hand these were deeply significant words. Both Christians and Jewish people will find themselves challenged by them when they realise that they were written in the light of the Holocaust and of the war which the newly created State of Israel found itself in. Buber had managed over the years to penetrate to the person and teaching of Jesus himself, getting behind the almost deafening message of the churches in their contempt for Jewish people and concerns.

We have a good record of Jesus' teachings, his power to heal the sick, his love for Israel and the world, and his mission to establish the Kingdom of Heaven. This record is found in the gospels, which form the heart of the New Testament. I know that it is common in some circles to find people rubbishing the gospels as not being trustworthy documents. They are written off as being too concerned with faith and not enough with history. Well, so are all the other Jewish works from the period. And of course all history is written from a particular point of view. The fact that the gospels were written by people who believed in Jesus does not mean that they are unacceptable as historical records of the life of Jesus.

To read the gospels is a remarkable experience. So many people assume that what they will find there will be irrelevant to modern life. In fact it is the contrary which is true: we hear Jesus speaking to our own day and age. Committed Christians who are used to applying Jesus' words to their own lives, on the other hand, will often miss the fact that to read the gospels is also to see Jesus speaking to us as a Jewish man of his own day and age. When Jewish people today read the gospels for themselves they find to their surprise that they can see Jesus there in his original context. What is more, some, like Buber, sense that Jesus could well have something to say to their own lives too.

So let's move on in this story of a Jewish rediscovery of Jesus.

This is a book written by a Christian who has come to know Jesus ben Joseph, Jesus the Galilean Jew of nearly 2,000 years ago, and who has also came to believe that Jesus is the Son of God, as presented in the New Testament. But Jewish readers needn't be afraid of an evangelical 'hard-sell'. There will be no attempt to offer any 'proofs' of Jesus' divinity, or the like. What I *do* hope is that people will read the gospels and encounter Jesus for themselves, but what they make of that encounter is between them and God.

When you do open the gospels and begin reading, you soon realise that a great deal of Jesus' life and teaching lies hidden to any person who doesn't appreciate the Jewishness of Jesus. In the next chapter we shall look at some aspects of this fact.

3

Jesus Was A Jew

There is a growing number of books being written on the Jewishness of Jesus, covering the whole range of relevant facts and perspectives. In this short chapter, my aim is to introduce just three areas in which it is necessary to see Jesus in his original Jewish milieu if we are to understand his life and teachings to the full. The three areas are the following: Jewish religious traditions, Jewish feasts, and Hebrew language and idioms. Much more than this could be examined, but I hope that enough will be presented within the scope of this book to alert the reader to the wealth of discovery that awaits whoever takes Jesus' indispensable Jewishness seriously.

Jewish Religious Traditions: We will look at two examples here, one an episode in Jesus' life, and the other an aspect of his teaching. In Matthew's gospel, we read about the following incident:

> Just then a woman who had suffered from
> haemorrhages for twelve years came up from
> behind and touched the edge of his cloak; for
> she said to herself, 'If I can only touch his
> cloak, I shall be healed.' (Matthew 9:20-21)

What picture do people imagine when they think of Jesus wearing a cloak? A bohemian artist figure? A Roman general? The classic old translation of the Bible called it the 'hem of Jesus' garment', and even though this is perhaps less misleading, it still does not convey what was really going on. To discover what Jesus was wearing, we must first read from the Hebrew Bible, from the book of Numbers:

> The LORD told Moses to say to the
> Israelites: 'Make tassels on the corners of your
> garments, you and your children's children.
> Into this tassel you are to work a violet
> thread, and whenever you see this in the
> tassel, you will remember all the LORD's
> commands and obey them.' (Numbers
> 15:37-39)

The Hebrew word for this 'tassel' is tzitzit, a word known by Jews the world over. The tassels themselves are also very familiar to the non-Jewish world. They are the four cords, as it were, which hang down from four points on what is today the Jewish prayer shawl (the 'tallit'). Jewish men who are faithful to the Torah of Moses wear a garment with these four tzitziot on it. Wearing it is a sign of devotion to God and faithfulness to the Torah, and of course it also serves as a sign to others that this man *is* such a devoted Jew.

This woman who came up behind Jesus leaned forward in the crowd to touch one of the tassels which hung down from his particular garment (perhaps an early form of prayer shawl, but we cannot be sure). Suffering as she did from chronic haemorrhaging, she would have been considered as 'unclean' by the Jewish religious authorities, and so rather than speak face-to-face with Jesus, and thereby risk an open confrontation in the crowd, she hoped to be healed anonymously, as it were. Reaching out to touch his tassels was not an act of magic, but rather a symbolic gesture of making contact not only with Jesus himself, but also, through him, with God, in obedience to whom Jesus wore the tassels in the first place.

To know this is to see the incident come alive. The whole episode is Jewish from first to last, portraying a scene of poignant devotion in the middle of a busy throng of people. There are many such scenes in the gospels which only reveal their full significance to those who appreciate the essential Jewishness of the characters (including Jesus) and the context.

But let us turn now to one of Jesus' teachings about morality and spirituality. It is worth pointing out that one of the characteristics of Jewish spirituality is the insistence that one's relationship with God cannot and must not be separated from everyday human relationships. A solid commitment to social justice and ethical behaviour in all aspects of life is regarded as a sure test of whether or not someone is in a proper relationship with God. Not surprisingly, we see this very characteristic in the teaching of Jesus.

The example I have chosen comes from Matthew's gospel, in a part where Jesus is speaking about the importance of right relationships between people.

> So if you are presenting your gift at the altar
> and suddenly remember that your brother has
> a grievance against you, leave your gift where
> it is before the altar. First go and make your
> peace with your brother; then come back and
> offer your gift. (Matthew 5:23-24)

Jesus' meaning is clear: there is no point in trying to sustain or restore a relationship with God while at the same time you have a broken relationship with another person. True worship and service of God can only exist within the context of real life here and now. To live as you please, ignoring what you are doing to others, and hoping to keep God in a secluded box, will simply not work in the Jewish understanding of true commitment.

However, the issue is more deliberate than even this. Note that Jesus is not speaking about a grievance we may have against someone else who has wronged us. He is drawing our attention to people who, rightly or wrongly, have a grievance against us. We are to seek them out and put things right before we can come to God with a clear conscience. This immediately reminds a Jewish person of that very insight within Judaism, an insight which has survived most especially in the religious tradition which relates to Yom Kippur, the Day of Atonement.

Here is a verse from the Mishnah, the authoritative legal commentary on the Hebrew Bible which forms the basis of the Talmud:

> For transgressions that are between man and
> God the Day of Atonement effects atonement,
> but for transgressions that are between a man
> and his fellow the Day of Atonement effects
> atonement only if he has appeased his fellow.
> (Yoma 8:9)

In Jewish tradition, rooted in this teaching of the first generations of rabbis, God will forgive anyone who genuinely repents on Yom Kippur and asks God to forgive him/her for sins committed against Him. However, God will *not* forgive anyone who has sinned against another person unless she/he also apologises to that other person and tries to sort out the damaged relationship. It is simply not acceptable to go quietly to the synagogue and in the silence confess to God that you have wronged someone. This was so important to the rabbis, that they developed a tradition of great profundity for the most solemn day of their year.

The tradition is that in the ten days between the Jewish New Year (Rosh HaShanah) and Yom Kippur every Jewish person must examine their behaviour and relationships over the past year and seek as far as possible to put things right. Jewish people still do this at the time of the New Year; they contact one another face-to-face, by phone, and by letter. Anyone who does not try to put things right is guilty of idolatry, in the sense that they have tried to create God in their own image. They are ignoring the true character of God and creating another one who will let them live their own lives, exactly as they please. They are also guilty of despising the other person, made as he/she is, in the image of God. Such a person will not receive the all-embracing forgiveness of God on Yom Kippur.

But on the other side, the rabbis also taught that should anyone come to you to apologise for something, and to ask for your forgiveness, you must give it willingly. No grudges are to be kept, and forgiveness is not to be withheld if the request is sincere. To refuse to forgive is to despise the loving, forgiving nature of God. You cannot withhold forgiveness from another human being and then ask God to ignore this fact and forgive you. These ten days in Jewish tradition are known as the 'Days of Awe', and it is a deeply moving experience to be aware of the seeking and granting of forgiveness which goes on in this time.

Jesus stands squarely within this tradition. He was not limiting himself to the specific commemoration of Yom Kippur, of course, but he speaks with a Jewish voice when he tells us all that before we presume to come close to God we must make sure that our family and social relationships are what they should be.

But let us turn now to a brief examination of three feasts which have an important place in the life and witness of Israel, and which provided Jesus with a wonderful medium through which to speak about his own life and witness.

Jewish Feasts: In a sense, the foundational feast in the Jewish calendar is that of Passover. In the same way, Christians present the service of Holy Communion, known by several names, as their foundational feast. Although the Communion service has, by and large, developed a life of its own within the Church, it really only makes sense within the context of the Jewish Passover meal and celebration. The eating of bread and drinking of wine are based on the actions and words of Jesus himself at what Christians refer to as 'the Last Supper'. What follows is the full text of that event as we find it recounted in Matthew's gospel:

> On the first day of Unleavened Bread the disciples came and asked Jesus, 'Where would you like us to prepare the Passover for you?' He told them to go to a certain man in the city with this message: 'The Teacher says, "My appointed time is near; I shall keep the Passover with my disciples at your house." ' The disciples did as Jesus directed them and prepared the Passover.

> In the evening he sat down with the twelve disciples; and during supper he said, 'Truly I tell you: one of you will betray me.' Greatly distressed at this, they asked him one by one, 'Surely you do not mean me, Lord?' He answered, 'One who has dipped his hand into the bowl with me will betray me. The Son of Man is going the way appointed for him in the Scriptures; but alas for that man by whom the Son of Man is betrayed! It would be

better for that man if he had never been born.'
Then Judas spoke, the one who was to betray him:
'Rabbi, surely you do not mean me?' Jesus replied,
'You have said it.'

During supper Jesus took bread, and having said
the blessing he broke it and gave it to the disciples
with the words: 'Take this and eat: this is my
body.' Then he took a cup, and having offered
thanks to God he gave it to them with the words:
'Drink from it, all of you. For this is my blood, the
blood of the covenant, shed for many for the
forgiveness of sins. I tell you, never again shall I
drink from this fruit of the vine until that day when
I drink it new with you in the kingdom of my
Father.'

After singing the Passover hymn, they went out to
the Mount of Olives.

There are several details in this account which are
worth mentioning, but even before that, it will be
obvious to any Jewish reader that we have a definite
Passover setting here for this most significant event
in the life of Jesus, the disciples, and indeed the
Church. Just how significant this is will become clear
as we examine the relevant matters.

First of all, let us remind ourselves of the fundamental religious issues of the Passover celebration. It
was no accident of history that Jesus chose the Passover week in order to inaugurate this central symbol
of the meaning of his life. As we shall see shortly,
there were other Jewish feasts which were not only
important to him, as they all would have been, but
which also afforded him an opportunity to communi-

cate something vital about his mission to Israel and the world. But it was the Passover which he chose for what is known as the Last Supper.

At Passover the Jewish people, then and now, celebrate their very foundation as the people of God. Not their call to be God's people, since that came with Abraham, but their emergence on the world stage as a self-consciously united and purposeful nation.

The Passover is about five truths:

a) It is about the God of Israel who keeps His promises in spite of everything. When the Israelites were suffering as slaves in Egypt it looked as if the great promises to Abraham were just a thing of the past. A failed dream. But God had not forgotten, nor was He turning His back on those commitments. He brought the Israelites out of Egypt in an act of historical proportions. The Exodus was a vindication of God's faithfulness.

b) It is about the God of Israel who really cares for His people.

There is a verse in the book of the Exodus which puts this very beautifully:

> The LORD said, 'I have witnessed the misery
> of my people in Egypt and have heard them
> crying out because of their oppressors. I know
> what they are suffering and have come down
> to rescue them ...' (Exodus 3:7-8)

c) It is about the God of Israel who has the power to deliver His people from all other powers, even those outside of the land of Israel. This is seen, of course, not only in the historical rescue from the land of Egypt, but also in the plagues, which demonstrated His power over the forces of nature and over those areas of life which the Egyptians considered the domains of their own gods.

d) It is about the God of Israel who graciously commits Himself in a covenant relationship to His people. His is a constant and consistent love for Israel. We see this in the fact that after the rescue of the Exodus He brings His people to Sinai and forms a new covenant with them there.

e) It is about the God of Israel who takes a mass of freed slaves and forms them into a nation to serve Him. This happened at Sinai where God gave them their national constitution, as it were, in the religious, ethical, and civil codes of the covenant. They were now to move in to live as a sovereign nation in the Promised Land.

All of this was, and is, celebrated at Passover time by Jewish people. And therefore all of this would have been in the minds of the disciples of Jesus as they came to Passover week and asked Jesus where he wished to celebrate the Passover. Let us note one or two details from the passage in Matthew which we looked at earlier. Note how it was simply taken for granted that Jesus would keep the Passover, like any other loyal Jewish person. His disciples asked casually where they were to celebrate, not whether they would celebrate.

Note also how we are told in passing that Jesus 'said the blessing' over the bread and 'offered thanks' for the wine. This is standard Jewish practice not to eat or drink without first reciting the appropriate blessing over the food and drink. What is more, there are set blessings for certain types of food, and would have been for the unleavened bread and the wine of the Passover meal. To this day there are still set blessings within the Passover liturgy, although they are not necessarily the same ones which were in use in Jesus' day, of course.

Christians need to realise that this was not simply an evening meal at which Jews talked about the Exodus. There was a meal, but it was set within the context of a whole liturgy celebrating the Exodus and the creation of Israel as a nation at Sinai. As well as eating a meal at the appropriate point in the evening, there are a number of symbolic foods and 'toasts' with the wine which serve as potent reminders of central truths of the Passover celebration.

For example, the bread was unleavened, as it was on the actual night of the Exodus, when the slaves fled from Egypt. At one point, a piece of this unleavened bread was broken off, and it was eaten after the meal as such was finished. I believe that it was this piece of unleavened bread, called the 'afikomen' in Jewish tradition, which Jesus lifted up and interpreted to his disciples as representing his own body, which was about to be broken in death for their sakes. This would have come as a terrible shock to them. Jewish tradition says that the afikomen was to represent the Passover lamb, and that this piece was eaten after the meal in order that the final taste of food should be in grateful memory of the lamb which was sacrificed at Passover. Now we can see the significance of Jesus' action and words.

What is more, after the meal Jesus 'took a cup' and related the wine in it to his own blood. Again, Christians need to realise that this was not simply Jesus helping himself to another drink.

During the Passover liturgy there are four prescribed moments when some wine is drunk in celebration of some aspect of Passover. The third of these comes after the meal, just as it is described in the gospels. It is known as the 'Cup of Redemption' in some Jewish traditions, and draws together in a toast, as it were, the focus on God's act of redemption. This was the cup which Jesus raised when he gave the interpretation that it also spoke of the coming act of redemption, when his blood would be spilled for the sake of his people.

The last section of the Passover celebration involves the singing of many songs of praise, centred around the singing of a set series of Psalms, Psalms 113–118. This collection of Psalms is known as the Hallel, coming from the same root as 'Halleluyah'.

Many translations of the New Testament end the passage which we looked at above with the words, 'After singing a hymn, they went out to the Mount of Olives.' This gives the impression, naturally enough, that they all joined in singing some piece by Luther, or Wesley, or the like. The translation I used is much better, in using the phrase, 'the Passover hymn', but of course the intended meaning was that Jesus and the disciples ended their celebration by singing the Hallel together.

38

By the way, it is to be highly recommended to all Christians to read through the Hallel in order to appreciate so much more profoundly the thoughts which were going through the minds of both Jesus and the disciples as they went to Gethsemane on the Mount of Olives!

There are more details which show this to have been a genuine Passover celebration, but this must suffice for the moment. To enter into the Jewishness of Jesus is to begin to appreciate him and his mission in its full depth. There could have been no more appropriate time or occasion for Jesus to give us this profound teaching. He found in it the perfect symbol of his life as the mediator of a New Exodus in which God would deliver His people from slavery to their own sin, and as the mediator of the New Covenant promised by the prophet Jeremiah, which would stand in continuity with the previous covenants, but also take them on much further.

There is even an ancient Jewish proverb which agrees that Passover would be the ideal time for the Messiah to come: 'In this night we were delivered; in this night we will be delivered.'(Mekhilta to Exodus 12:42)

We turn now to a different Jewish feast. One of the most popular of these is the feast of Hannukah, which takes place, according to the western calendar, in the month of December. This is one of the feasts which is not mentioned, let alone commanded, in the Hebrew Bible. The roots of this celebration go back to the days between the events of the Hebrew Bible and the New Testament when Israel was under the terrible yoke of the Greek-dominated Syrian empire.

As part of their campaign of total control in the country, the Syrians desecrated the temple in Jerusalem. They realised, as many tyrants have throughout history, that in order to crush the spirit of any nation or people, you must ridicule and desecrate their religious beliefs and central symbols. Therefore they wreaked havoc in the Jerusalem temple. They were determined to destroy the Jewish faith. Eventually, a family of faithful Jews led a successful revolt against the Syrian forces, and, against all the odds, drove them out of Jerusalem and re-dedicated the temple. The Hebrew term for dedication or re-dedication is 'hannukah', which explains the name of the feast.

The story is recounted in the Apocrypha, in the first book of the Maccabees. Christians, of course, tend to be not only ignorant of this book and its story, but also indifferent to it. In one of the verses of the story, we are told that it was the very family which led the successful revolt against the Syrians who initiated this annual feast in memory of the day when God worked a great miracle and gave them a remarkable victory over yet another world power and oppressor.

> After that Judah, his brothers and the whole congregation of Israel decreed that the re-dedication of the altar should be celebrated with joy and gladness each year at the same season, for eight days, from the twenty-fifth day of the month of Kislev. (1 Maccabees 4:59)

In summary, then, the feast of Hannukah celebrates the liberation of the Jewish people from the yoke of an empire which sought to enslave them and destroy their religious faith in the God of Israel. It was (and very much still is) an extremely important and popular festival period. The Jewish people in Jesus' day would have been very interested in what he made of it. We today should be just as interested! And so we have here another case of needing to know the Jewishness of Jesus in order to fully appreciate an episode in his life which is recounted in the gospels.

In John's gospel, we read the following:

> It was winter, and the festival of the
> Dedication was being held in Jerusalem. As
> Jesus was walking in the temple precincts, in
> Solomon's Portico, the Jews gathered around
> him and asked: 'How long are you going to
> keep us in suspense? Tell us plainly: are you
> the Messiah?' (John 10:22-24)

The full import of this question only becomes apparent when we know the Jewish context of this particular winter festival. Four points can be made from these few verses in John. Note first of all that the action takes place in Jerusalem itself. Jesus is there for the feast. Secondly, we note that he is very much involved with what is going on, since he is walking in the precincts of the temple at the time when the dedication of the temple was foremost in the mind of the Jewish people.

The next point to note, however, is, again, one which casual reading of the text would miss. John makes a point of telling us that Jesus was walking in the area known as Solomon's Portico.

Why should this be significant? It was a part of the outer court of Herod's temple which ran around the eastern side of the temple complex, and was probably constructed entirely by Herod's own architects and building teams. Herod, it will be remembered, was appointed as 'King of Judea' by the Romans, and ruled over Judea as their man on the spot, and with their blessing and protection. Herod was therefore a symbol to faithful Jews of the fact that once again the Jewish people and the land of Israel were under the yoke of a foreign power.

This brings us to the fourth point, which is this: Jewish people were once more pleading with God to deliver them from this oppression. But this time there was a difference in that many were desperately asking God to deliver them once-and-for-all from the cycle of destruction and deliverance. In short, there was a Messianic cry in the air. Would *this* be the time when God would send the Messiah to rid the country of its oppressor and then establish Israel as His nation on earth?

Therefore the question to Jesus: 'Tell us plainly: are you the Messiah?' There was a specific context for this question, and without it we lose too much.

I would like to look now at a third Jewish feast which played a vital role in Jesus' life and teaching. This is a Biblical feast which is celebrated in the autumn season, and is known in English by several names, the commonest of them being the feast of Tabernacles. Tabernacles (Sukkot, in Hebrew) celebrates two things. On the one hand, it is the time of the gathering of the crops from the fields and the orchards in Israel, and so serves as a kind of harvest thanksgiving festival.

On the other hand, the name refers to the huts, or tabernacles, in which the Israelites lived during their forty years of wandering in the wilderness between the time of the Exodus and their entry into the Promised Land. It therefore serves as a reminder of two spiritual truths to the Jewish people. Firstly that they are dependent on God for His protection, and secondly that God can be depended on even in times of trouble, since the forty years of wandering was itself a punishment from God, and yet even then He was looking after them. Tabernacles is one of the three most important festivals in Jewish life, along with Passover and Pentecost, at which time adult male Jews were commanded in the Bible to make pilgrimage to Jerusalem (see Exodus 34:23-24).

We now read from John's gospel once more.

> After that Jesus travelled around within
> Galilee;...But when the Jewish feast of
> Tabernacles was close at hand, his brothers
> said to him, 'You should leave here and go
> into Judaea, so that your disciples may see the
> great things you are doing.' ...
>
> When the festival was already half over, Jesus
> went up to the temple and began to teach...
>
> On the last and greatest day of the festival
> Jesus stood and declared, 'If anyone is thirsty,
> let him come to me and drink. Whoever

believes in me, as scripture says, "Streams of
living water shall flow from within him." He
was speaking of the Spirit which believers in
him would later receive ...

Once again Jesus addressed the people: 'I am
the light of the world. No follower of mine
shall walk in darkness; he shall have the light
of life.' (John 7:1-3, 14, 37-39; 8:12)

Here we are faced once more with a need to appreciate something about a Jewish feast before we can
fully recover the impact of Jesus' words. There are
two things in particular which I wish to highlight in
this short treatment of the feast. One of the more
spectacular aspects of the feast in Biblical times was
the drawing of water every morning from the Pool of
Siloam, its transfer in a ceremonial procession in a
golden pitcher to the altar in the temple, and its
being poured out as an offering to God along with the
offering of wine.

This was an especially potent symbol of the
people's trust in God. Tabernacles occurs at the end
of the long dry summer, when there is a desperate
need for rain for the coming year's crops.

Indeed part of the festival of Tabernacles to this
day is the formal offering of prayer for rain. It was
therefore an act of great trust that God would answer
those prayers and send rain to pour out a large
pitcher of precious water at that time of the year!

Now we can see the significance of the fact that
Jesus chose this festival as the time to proclaim that
believing in him would lead to a life-transforming

relationship. He used that very imagery of water as the prerequisite for life: 'If anyone is thirsty, let him come to me and drink.' There would be no need to turn to the natural spring outside the walls of Jerusalem for water: to believe in Jesus is to have 'streams of living water' bubbling up within you. What a powerful statement this must have been! But there is one other aspect of the feast of Tabernacles which proved just as powerful when transformed by Jesus into a symbol pointing to himself. The temple's 'courtyard of the women' was lit with four hundred lamps which were set up on high columns.

According to Jewish traditional sources the light from this courtyard illuminated all the homes and courtyards in Jerusalem.

Men danced around with large torches to accentuate this theme that God was the giver of light.

And so we can now also see the significance of Jesus' words at that time: 'I am the light of the world. No follower of mine shall walk in darkness; he shall have the light of life.' That must have been an exceptionally dramatic moment!

I hope, then, that something has been seen in these three examples of the need to appreciate the Jewishness of Jesus in order to appreciate Jesus himself. Finally, let us look at the issue of the actual language of Jesus.

Hebrew Language and Idioms: One or two of the many instances will suffice to make the point here that much of what Jesus said is lost unless his mother tongue of Hebrew is understood to be the original language of not only Jesus but also the first disciples.

Here are two famous and troublesome verses from Matthew's gospel:

> The lamp of the body is the eye. If your eyes
> are sound, you will have light for your whole
> body; if your eyes are bad, your whole body
> will be in darkness. (Matthew 6:22-23)

What does it mean to have 'sound' or 'bad' eyes? As a matter of fact, the original text here has the singular phrase, 'If your eye is good'. What can this mean? Well, it is a literal translation of a Hebrew idiom. When someone is said to have a good eye, it means that he/she is a generous person. Correspondingly, to have a bad eye is to be mean-spirited. Jesus is saying that if you have a generous disposition, an open and welcoming attitude to life, then you will find that life is good and worth living.

On the other hand, if you are a person with a mean disposition, then perhaps you will find that life seems dark and unwelcoming to you.

Another type of example altogether can be found in the opening chapter of Matthew's gospel. This gospel opens with seventeen verses of genealogy to introduce Jesus to the readers. This in itself seems irrelevant and boring to many Christians today, but of course in its Jewish setting it would have been absolutely imperative to show the ancestry and 'pedigree' of Jesus as one of the pieces of evidence for his Messianic credentials. But let us look a little closer at the genealogy itself.

It is organised by Matthew into three sections of

fourteen generations each. The final verse of the
opening section reads as follows:

> There were thus fourteen generations in all
> from Abraham to David, fourteen from David
> until the deportation to Babylon, and fourteen
> from the deportation until the Messiah.
> (Matthew 1:17)

These three focal points are extremely important.
Abraham was the man chosen by God to be the one
through whom the whole people of Israel were called
to be God's chosen people. The Abrahamic covenant
followed this fundamental call of the people of God,
and was the basis of their relationship with Him.
David was the king chosen by God to be the one
through whom the Messianic line would proceed.
The Exile in Babylon stood as a symbol of the suffering and disenfranchising of the Jewish people by a
sequence of conquering powers who wished to control the fertile crescent which linked the two land
masses of Africa and Asia. Jesus was a true son of all
three, fully identified with the covenant people, the
Davidic lineage, and the terrible plight of his people.

But there is still a 'hidden' message in this genealogy. Matthew has written it in a code which is only
apparent to those with knowledge of Hebrew. In
Hebrew the letters of the alphabet double up as the
numbers. In other words, the first letter of the alphabet is also the number one, etc. This of course means
that every word, every sentence, every verse in the
Bible, etc., has a numerical value which is found by
adding up the sum total of the letters to be found in

it. In many Jewish religious circles this is held to be of considerable significance.

Since King David was the first in the royal line of the Messiah, the Messiah is often referred to by the title, 'son of David', or even simply by the name, 'David'. The numerical value of the name is fourteen—hence the stress on the three sets of fourteen generations. The very structure of the genealogy is a coded message that Jesus was believed to be the Messiah.

Thus we see that even the language of Jesus and the gospels is sometimes a closed book to us unless we remember to let Jesus speak to us from his own Hebrew world.

What have we discovered in this chapter? That the Jewish and Christian attempts to present Jesus as other than Jewish are the product, not of scholarship nor of honest spirituality, but of ignorance or prejudice. There can be no denying the fact: Jesus was a Jew!

4

Jewish Re-discoveries Of A Jewish Jesus

Most Jewish people who speak to me about their religious ideas and values are frightened to consider Jesus very seriously. What little talk about him there might have been in their family homes or education has tended to paint a picture of Jesus as a deluded charlatan who deceived Jews into thinking that he could work miracles of healing, and that he could bring them closer to God.

Further, he is presented as having been responsible for all the crimes committed against the Jewish people by the Church. To even wonder whether he actually brought the offer of truth and life to Israel is seen as an act of betrayal of the memory of the Jewish martyrs who suffered at the hands of crusaders and grand inquisitors. Jesus is, quite simply, not a popular source of conversation in most Jewish homes.

But in actual fact there are Jewish people who are beginning to take Jesus seriously. Significant Jewish scholars are publishing books and articles in which

49

they are urging their fellow Jews to discover just how Jewish Jesus is. Indeed for some time now there has been what some call a Jewish 'reclaiming' of Jesus, leading in no small measure to a new confidence even among more liberal Christian scholars that the historical Jesus can indeed be found in the gospels.

There have been some particular landmarks along the way. In the next chapter we shall take a look at some extended passages from the works of both Jewish and Christian scholars in order to get a clearer picture of their understanding of Jesus the Jew, but for the moment it will be useful to highlight some of the outstanding *Jewish* contributions to Jesus research in the past century. At the end of the 19th century, in 1894, Claude Montefiore, a leading British thinker of the liberal Jewish movement, said of Jesus that he was

> The most important Jew who ever lived...whose life and character have been regarded by almost all the best and wisest people...as the greatest religious exemplar of every age.[2]

It must be conceded, of course, that Montefiore (1858–1938) did not represent the consensus within the Jewish community. His extreme liberalism put him on the fringes of mainstream Jewish life, and of course it was his break with the traditional Jewish attitudes and practices which made it at all possible for him to consider Jesus in a clear light. Nonetheless, this statement made a great impact on the Jewish community. However, the real watershed came in 1922, when Joseph Klausner (1874-1958), the Professor of Hebrew Literature at the Hebrew University, wrote the ground-breaking modern book on Jesus by a Jewish scholar. His Hebrew original was translated into English in 1925 by Herbert Danby, and it took the Jewish (and Christian!) world by storm. At one summary point he wrote:

> Jesus is a great teacher of morality and an artist in parable. He is the moralist for whom, in the religious light, morality counts as everything: in his ethical code there is a sublimity, a distinctiveness and an originality in form unparalleled in any other Hebrew ethical code.[3]

These words were considered scandalous by many Jewish authorities, especially among the Orthodox communities. Klausner's book was published before the rise of the Nazi movement in Germany, of course, but a generation later, in 1950, Buber presented his own opinion of Jesus to the post-Holocaust Jewish world. A fuller quote than was given earlier will indicate the extent to which Buber was taking the issue further than had previously been the case.

> From my youth onwards I have found in Jesus my great brother. That Christianity has regarded and does regard him as God and Saviour has always appeared to me a fact of the highest importance which, for his sake and my own, I must endeavour to understand ... I am more than certain that a great place belongs to him in Israel's history of faith and that this place cannot be described by any of the usual categories.[4]

By 1973, after yet another generation, Geza Vermes, one of the world's leading specialists on the Dead Sea Scrolls, was able to conclude from his investigations into the life of Jesus that

> no objective and enlightened student of the Gospels can help but be struck by the incomparable superiority of Jesus ... Second to none in profundity of insight and grandeur of character.[5]

Finally, one must mention Pinchas Lapide, a contemporary Orthodox theologian who is a specialist in the area of Jewish-Christian relations. In a now famous 1981 book he made the declaration that

> Jesus is no longer the central figure in the discussion between church and synagogue. Thanks to the current surge of interest in Jesus within the State of Israel, the Nazarene, long shrouded in silence, is beginning to be acknowledged among his own people and in his own land.[6]

These kinds of statements would have been unthinkable for Jewish people before the modern period, and even now, most Jewish people advise a more cautious appreciation of Jesus, lest the Jewish community develop the wrong attitude to *Christianity*, namely that it too is acceptable for Jewish people. However, Jesus himself is very definitely back on the agenda in Jewish-Christian relations. It is my hope that more and more Jewish people will also begin to think again about him.

Christians tend to want to focus on what is unique

about Jesus, stressing what is distinctive about him, what makes him stand out from his context. This is understandable and acceptable, since Jesus is the centre of their lives, and the one who has made all the difference to them in their relationship with God. But even Christians need to learn that if they wish to find out all they can about Jesus, then they must also accept that there would have been ordinary aspects of his life which were also characteristic of him. What a person inherits and accepts from his/her heritage, and from the insights of her/his contemporaries, is as much characteristic of that person as the distinct contributions that he/she makes to society. No one— not even Jesus—lives in a vacuum if they are human at all.

Too many sermons are preached in churches which give the impression that Jesus invented the parable, for instance. The fact is that teaching in parables is found in many cultures, and the Jewish culture is no exception. Jewish religious teachers, including the Rabbis, used this form of communication and instruction constantly, and to good effect. Some of Jesus' parables are quite outstanding, but not because they were the only ones on offer.

To raise another matter: was Jesus the first Jewish person to ever teach that God could be called Father? Does the Aramaic term, Abba, necessarily denote an intimacy which was missing from the spiritual life of Jewish people in Jesus' day? There is still a huge debate about these matters among the specialists, and yet it is commonplace to hear Christian sermons in which it is presented as beyond question that Jesus initiated this close type of relationship with God. Other examples could be given where the desire to present Jesus as original in everything he said and did has stepped beyond the boundary of *knowledge* to the world of what-we-would-like-to-be-true.

In other words, not everything that Jesus said and did was necessarily without precedent, or resulted in shock and amazement. Surely he enjoyed playing games with other children when he was a young boy? I'm sure he didn't win every time in every game even though he was Jesus! He presumably had favourite food, like most of us. He would have had favourite walks in the Galilean hills and favourite songs, etc.

From another perspective, it must also be said that Jesus' own ministry was carried out in the context of God's revelation to, and relationship with, Israel. Many of the Jewish people recognised that he taught and lived in the light of the Messianic promises of the Hebrew Bible. The extent to which this is true is not always appreciated these days, however. One example will suffice. In Mark's gospel we find an account of an incident in which the friends of a man who was paralysed from the waist down brought him on a bed (what we might think of as a stretcher of sorts) to be healed by Jesus. Such was the crowd, that they had to go to quite some trouble to get to Jesus.

> When he saw their faith, Jesus said to the man, 'My son, your sins are forgiven.' Now there were some scribes sitting there, thinking to themselves, 'How can the fellow talk like that? It is blasphemy! Who but God can

forgive sins?'

Jesus knew at once what they were thinking,
and said to them, 'Why do you harbour such
thoughts? Is it easier to say to this paralysed
man, "Your sins are forgiven," or to say,
"Stand up, take your bed, and walk"? But to
convince you that the Son of Man has
authority on earth to forgive sins'—he turned
to the paralysed man—'I say to you, stand
up, take your bed, and go home.'

And he got up, and at once took his bed and
went out in full view of them all, so that they
were astounded and praised God. 'Never
before', they said, 'have we seen anything like
this.' (Mark 2:5–12)

To understand the real impact of this incident, we
must remind ourselves of a fundamental teaching in
the Hebrew Bible about the power of God. In Biblical Hebrew, the word for 'a word' and the word for 'a
deed' are identical (the Hebrew term is davar). This
reveals a very rich vein of theology in the Jewish
faith. It means that as far as God is concerned, words
and deeds are virtually the same. To put it another
way, as far as God is concerned, when He speaks and
says that He will do something, it is as good as done
already.

Evidence of this can be found throughout the
Hebrew Bible, but nowhere more gloriously than in
the very opening chapter of Genesis. The majestic
transcendence of God the Creator, in contrast with
the way the gods of the other ancient near eastern

nations were presented as creating the world, is perfectly expressed in the way that He actually goes about creating the heavens and the earth. Israel's God does not need to get His hands dirty. He merely says the words, and the deeds follow automatically. The formula of Genesis 1 is well known:

God said, 'Let there be light,' and there was light …

God said, 'Let there be a vault between the waters' … and so it was.

God said, 'Let the water under the heavens be gathered into one place' … and so it was.

God said, 'Let the earth produce growing things' … So it was.

God said, 'Let there be lights' … So it was.

God said, 'Let the water teem with living creatures, and let birds fly above the earth' … God said, 'Let the earth bring forth living creatures' … So it was.

Then God said, 'Let us make human beings in our image' … So it was.

This marvellous presentation of the power of God's word is echoed in different ways throughout the Hebrew Bible. Isaiah has a beautiful passage in which God says:

As the rain and snow come down from the
heavens and do not return there without
watering the earth, making it produce grain to
give seed for sowing and bread to eat, so it is
with my word issuing from my mouth; it will
not return to me empty without
accomplishing my purpose and succeeding in
the task for which I sent it. (Isaiah 55: 10-11.
See also, for example, Jeremiah 5:14; Psalm
148: 1-6)

The men and women who were listening to Jesus on
the occasion of the healing of the paralysed man,
were Jews for whom this was a basic part of their
belief about God. But we need to look even more
closely at Jesus' Jewish context than this. According
to the Hebrew Bible, God's *prophets* are His mes-
sengers, or better still, His ambassadors. They speak
for Him. In other words, a true prophet also has the
gift of this power, whereby his words are as good as
done as soon as he speaks to them. This was why
people feared the words of the prophets, and
nowhere is this seen more graphically (and enter-
tainingly), than in the account of the prophet Balaam.

While the Israelites were still on their way to the
Promised Land after the Exodus, the Moabites pan-
icked at their presence in their lands. Their king,
Balak, decided to procure the services of a prophet to
curse Israel. This in itself shows that prophets were
indeed held to have the gift of 'making words come
true'. If Israel had been cursed by Balaam, then the
curse would have been effective in real life too. However, as we read in the book of Numbers, God had

other ideas from Balak. He intended to *bless* Israel, and so gives Balaam only words of blessing. Needless to say, this infuriates Balak, because he knows that nothing can now prevent Israel from being blessed. This is the power of the word of God, and the word of His prophet. Balak's responses are well worth enjoying! He sends a message to Balaam:

> Come at once and lay a curse on them, because they are too many for me. I may then be able to defeat them and drive them out of the country. I know that those whom you bless are blessed, and those whom you curse are cursed ... God said to Balaam, 'You are not to curse the people, because they are to be blessed.' ... Balak said, 'What is this you have done? I sent for you to put a curse on my enemies, and what you have done is to bless them.' ... Then Balak said to Balaam, 'You will not put a curse on them; then at least do not bless them.' (Numbers 22:6, 12; 23:11, 25)

So we see that the crowd who were listening to Jesus had also been brought up with this belief that a true prophet would have the power to do what he said he would do. In fact this is not quite true. There are two other passages which we must look at before we are able to return to the episode of the paralysed man.

Israel was well aware of the fact that there was a need to be able to discern between true and false prophets. On the one hand, there would be people who would claim to have the power of 'word and deed', but who would not in fact have it. On the other hand, there would be those who might seem to have that power, but who would not be prophets of God, and who would seek to entice Israel to follow other gods.

And so we must now turn to two important passages in the book of Deuteronomy which give Israel directions on how to test the claims of a possible prophet.

> Should a prophet or a pedlar of dreams appear among you and offer you a sign or a portent, and call on you to go after other gods whom you have not known and to worship them, even if the sign or portent should come true do not heed the words of that prophet or dreamer.

> If you wonder, 'How are we to recognise a word that the LORD has not uttered?' here is the answer: When a word spoken by a prophet in the name of the LORD is not fulfilled and does not come true, it is not a word spoken by the LORD. (Deuteronomy 13:1-3; 18:21-22)

Here, then, is the tension in the air on that day in Capernaum when Jesus healed the paralysed man. Was Jesus a true prophet or not? Did he have the power to turn words into deeds? Would the people who saw his power, if he should turn out to have it, turn to follow other gods? And so we can now understand all that was going on in that episode. In response to a plea for physical healing Jesus pronounces that the man's sins were forgiven. The scribes were right, of course, that it is only God who can forgive sins. Was Jesus a blasphemer, trying to lead them into idolatry of some sort?

Although Jesus uses the term 'son' when announcing the man's forgiveness, as though speaking for their Father God, and not just for himself; and although Jesus speaks in the passive mood ('your sins are forgiven'), as though he is announcing a state already achieved by the man, rather than actively saying, 'I forgive you', the scribes nevertheless sensed something more than mere announcement by Jesus. They knew that Jesus was saying something provocative and profound.

So what did he say? We need to pay particular attention here to Jesus' actual words. He did not say to his challengers, 'Is it easier to do the forgiving or the healing?' He asked them whether it was easier to *say the words* about forgiving or healing. Most of the Christian commentators on this episode have missed the point altogether. The fact is that words are cheap! It is as easy to say, 'Your sins are forgiven' as it is to say, 'You are healed'. The question is, how would you know? Jesus could say to the man that his sins were forgiven by God, but it would be unverifiable by the people who heard this word.

And so we see the wisdom of Jesus when he says that to convince them that he does in fact have the authority to pronounce the forgiveness of sins, he will speak another word which *will* be verifiable. If he says that the man is healed and the man then gets up and walks home, then the scribes and everyone else will see that Jesus has the power to heal. This in turn will give them confidence that when he says he has the authority to pronounce forgiveness, he does in fact have that power.

Jesus has the power of God, as they all see when the paralysed man is healed. Jesus has the authority for the forgiveness of sins as they all realise too. But will this lead to a desertion of God? On the contrary, the people 'were astounded and praised God'.

Mark 2 can obviously be read with benefit by someone who is unaware of this set of contexts, but the full power of the incident is only evident when we try to see this miracle of healing *within* Jesus' Jewish context, rather than if we quickly understand it as lifting Jesus out of all context altogether.

But none of this detracts from Jesus' greatness or uniqueness.

Perhaps it would be useful to compare it to studying a contour model of a region. It is only when you see the full context of an area that you can really appreciate the significance of any particular place. How high is a hill in comparison with the hills around it, etc? Mere maps may not convey the answer with the same power as study of the contours of a scale model. In the same way, it is important to know the whole person, Jesus, not just the extraordinary aspects of his life, in order to fully appreciate his uniqueness.

Not surprisingly, Jewish people who do think about Jesus tend to want to focus on the ordinary, or readily acceptable, aspects of his life. They concentrate on those aspects which they can easily interpret within the common context of Jewish life in general at that time and place. There is a desire to reduce Jesus, as many Christians would say, to the level of being a loyal Jew of his generation—perhaps even a *great* Jew—but no more. The Jewish scholars whom we have looked at in this chapter certainly all believe, in spite of the differences among them, that Jesus was a creative genius whose greatness transcends his own generation.

But none of them would give any credence to Christian claims that he was divine as well as human, or that his death on the cross was the means of the world's salvation.

What are we to say, then? Both aspects of Jesus' life are needed in order to fully appreciate him; he is unknowable outside of his particular Jewish context, and yet he cannot be placed in a box which says 'First Century Jew', and left there. Jesus transcends all such attempts to domesticate him. Having said that, though, it is vital to know Jesus the Jew. Thankfully, a large number of writers and teachers are seeking to help the Church rediscover its Jewish roots. Although I hope that the present book will also be able to play a part in that task, I am seeking in particular to help the Jewish community to become more aware of those Jewish writers and teachers who are trying to restore Jesus to that community's own history.

Ultimately, then, this little book is an encouragement to Jewish people to let Jesus speak to them for himself.

5

Jesus Was Not A Christian

One major issue which has been stressed so far in this book is that Jesus cannot be fully appreciated if he is uprooted from his human—Jewish—life. Albert Schweitzer, more generally remembered today as a pioneering medical missionary to Africa, saw this clearly as he worked on his book about the modern Church's search for the historical Jesus. Schweitzer pointed out that having tried to make Jesus into simply a contemporary figure for modern times, scholars had been forced to concede that Jesus

> does not stay; He passes by our time and returns to his own.[7]

A Roman Catholic writer has recently said that the Church must not try to deny or ignore its Jewish roots, and especially not the Jewishness of Jesus, since its own identity is at stake.

> We Christians cannot understand ourselves
> accurately if our self-interpretation is
> fundamentally at odds with the truth of our
> beginnings.[8]

Indeed, there is currently a real danger that some Christians, unless they are careful to study their roots properly, will be deceived into seeing Jesus not as a Jew at all, but as simply a 'Palestinian'. There is a definite programme being pursued by some Arab/ Palestinian Christians to counter the Church's search for its Jewish roots, by trying to present Jesus as more akin to the Arab Palestinian people. One leading Arab theologian writes:

> Jesus was born in Bethlehem, grew up in Nazareth,
> was baptized in the Jordan river ... the first
> witnesses to the Resurrection were Palestinians; the
> Church was born in Palestine as the early disciples
> and followers of Jesus were Palestinians ... The
> Palestinian Christians of today are the descendants
> of those early Christians.

> I am a Palestinian Christian. I am a descendant of
> the first Christians in the world, and Jesus Christ
> was born in my country, in my land.[9]

Certain Jewish people might have preferred it had Jesus not been Jewish, since they wish, as we have seen, to disassociate themselves from anything which they see as Christian. Certain Christians might choose to ignore the Jewishness of Jesus because of their latent anti-Jewishness or their determination to locate Jesus in a cultural vacuum. But the fact remains stubbornly present: Jesus was not European; he was not Palestinian Arab—he was Palestinian Jewish. Anchoring Jesus where he actually belongs helps us to resist the temptation to create him in our own image.

Let us look at another example of how easy it is for a modern person, especially a non-Jewish person, to read something about Jesus and assume that Jesus' words can be fully understood without any recourse to their original context. So often this becomes, in effect, a creating of Jesus in the reader's image. One of the most important teachings of Jesus comes in direct response to a question put to him by one of a group of Pharisees who were keen to try to ascertain what was the heart of Jesus' faith. The Pharisee asked Jesus:

> 'Teacher, which is the greatest commandment
> in the law?' He answered, 'Love the Lord
> your God with all your heart, with all your
> soul, and with all your mind.' That is the
> greatest, the first commandment. The second
> is like it: 'Love your neighbour as yourself.'
> Everything in the law and the prophets hangs
> on these two commandments.' (Matthew
> 22:34-40)

I have heard many sermons over the years in which the preachers have interpreted this passage in such a way as to show that Jesus was not at all a typical Jewish man. A typical Jewish man, they say, would have resisted any attempt to reduce the Law to one or two commandments. Instead, this reply of Jesus' is taken to be an attack on what the preacher invariably describes as the Pharisaic obsession with the Law. Jesus, according to this non-Jewish, and, as often as not, anti-Jewish image, was telling the Pharisees that Law had no real place in a relationship with God. Any true relationship with God depends solely on loving God and on loving one another. Love, not Law, is the important thing. This is a typical and unacceptable 'image' of Jesus, the two Testaments of the Bible, Judaism, and Christianity. It has, in fact, become the type of image we call a caricature.

There are two things to be said about this particular issue before we move on in the chapter. Firstly, we have no reason at all to doubt that the Pharisees themselves, as the Rabbis after them, also liked to crystallize and summarize the commandments in terms of the essence of God's desired response from His people.

We actually have some texts to this very effect in the early rabbinic teachings and traditions. For example, in the Talmud, we find the following passage:

> Rabbi Simlai said: 'Six hundred and thirteen
> commandments were given to Moses; three
> hundred and sixty five negative commandments …
> and two hundred and forty eight positive
> commandments … Then David came and reduced
> them to eleven. Then Isaiah came and reduced
> them to six. Then Micah came and reduced them
> to three. Then Isaiah came again and reduced them
> to two … Then Amos came and reduced them to

one ... Or you could also say Habakkuk came and reduced them to one. (Makkot 23b-24a)

This wonderful passage does not mean that there was any attempt by the Rabbis to try to bypass the commandments. Nor were they really saying that only a handful of the commandments were of any importance. They were doing what Jesus was doing—helping the Jewish people to get some sense of the overall perspective and thrust of the commandments of God for their lives. The texts that Rabbi Simlai was referring to are not quoted in the Talmud, because the readers knew them well enough themselves. But I'll list them all here so that we can see something of the various expressions of the essence of the will of God.

> LORD, who may lodge in your tent? Who may dwell on your holy mountain?
> *One of blameless life,*
> *who does what is right*
> *and speaks the truth from his heart;*
> *who has no malice on his tongue,*
> *who never wrongs his fellow,*
> *and tells no tales against his neighbour;*
> *who shows his scorn for those the LORD rejects,*
> *but honours those who fear the LORD;*
> *who holds to his oath even to his own hurt,*
> *who does not put his money out to usury,*
> *and never accepts a bribe against the innocent.*
> He who behaves in this way will remain unshaken.
> (Psalm 15, giving David's 11 commands)
> The person who:

> *behaves uprightly*
> *and speaks the truth,*
> *who scorns to enrich himself by extortion,*
> *who keeps his hands clean from bribery,*
> *who stops his ears against talk of murder*
> *and closes his eyes against looking at evil—*

he it is who will dwell on the heights, his refuge a fastness in the cliffs, his food assured and water never failing him. (Isaiah 33:15-16, giving his 6 commands)

The LORD has told you mortals what is good, and what it is that the LORD requires of you:
only to act justly,
to love loyalty,
to walk humbly with your God.
(Micah 6:8, giving his 3 commands)

These are the words of the LORD:
Maintain justice,
and do what is right;
for my deliverance is close at hand, and my victory will soon be revealed.
(Isaiah 56:1, giving his 2 commands)

These are the words of the LORD to the people of Israel:
If you would live, *make your way to me.* (Amos 5:4)

The righteous will live by faith. (Habakkuk 2:4)

Now when the Pharisee asked Jesus for his opinion on which was the greatest commandment, he was concerned to hear how Jesus would characterize the essence of the commandments. This would be an important way of testing whether or not Jesus' theology was sound. In other words Jesus did not do something untoward here, but responded in a natural and proper way to the question. He was not rejecting the commandments, or belittling the place of laws and principles in the life of a true believer in God.

This brings us to the second point to be made. It really is no longer acceptable for Christians to preserve the image of the Jewish community, Judaism as a faith, and the very Hebrew Bible itself, as characterised by 'Law', thus contrasting the image of the New Testament and all things Christian as having to do only with 'Love'. In the first place, the covenant relationship between God and Israel is clearly presented in the Hebrew Bible as based on God's love for Israel, not at all on whether or not Israel is obedient to the laws of God. The very text which Jesus refers to as giving the greatest commandment (love the LORD your God with all your heart and soul and mind), is one of many which place love for God at the centre of Israel's response to Him.

In the second place, there is plenty of law in the New Testament.

Here are two words from Jesus himself, and one each from James and John, two of the early leaders in the movement of believers in Jesus:

> If you love me, you will obey what I
> command ... You are my friends if you do
> what I command ... ... faith without deeds
> is dead ... This is how we know that we love
> the children of God: by loving God and
> carrying out his commands. (John 14:15;

15:14; James 2:26; 1 John 5:2)

The Bible is clear that in God's eyes there is no division of life into either obedience to His law or love. Both are required by God. Therefore Jesus is not responding to the Pharisee by saying that in his view love must supersede law. On the contrary, Jesus acknowledges that loving God and loving one's neighbour are both in fact *commanded* by God. Jesus' two commandments are taken from the Hebrew Bible, specifically from Deuteronomy 6:5 and from Leviticus 19:18.

This, then, has been but one example of how people can ignore the Jewish context of Jesus' life and produce an interpretation of his words or actions which are really a way, intentional or not, of creating him in an image which suits them. As I have said, anchoring Jesus where he actually belongs helps us to resist the temptation to create him in our own image.

What do we know, then, about the world in which Jesus lived? His world was one of great turmoil and frustration. What were the Jewish people to make of the fact that the Promised Land was under the oppressive rule of the pagan Romans? As in all situations where one people occupies the land and life of another, there were incidents of violent aggression between Roman soldiers and Jewish resisters. The taxation system was corrupt and crippling.

Some Jews withdrew into lives of desperate prayer, pleading with God to intervene, and to liberate the Jewish people and the land of Israel from the yoke of oppression. Others formed various sorts of resistance movements and tried to force God's hand into doing something.

In amongst all this fervour was the persistent faith and hope that God would send the longed-for Messiah to lead the people of Israel in the journey to their destiny. This would be a holy war, in which the Messiah would lead them to victory over the selfishness of their own lives, and also to freedom from all other forms of bondage. But when would he come? Turmoil, hope, and frustration. This is the world to which Jesus came, and we are beginning to see Jesus in the proper context when we acknowledge that.

But having said that, it remains true that different scholars see Jesus quite differently even when they agree that he can only be understood as a first-century Jew. From *Christian* commentators have come presentations of Jesus which understand him primarily as an aggressive, political, Jewish revolutionary, intent on ridding the Promised Land of the Roman oppressors; or as a philosopher in the style of the Cynics; or as a committed advocate for the poor and exploited; or as a prophet who believed that he was living in the last days before the coming final judgement of God; or even as a wonder-working magician who wandered around the Jewish settlements encouraging them to have faith in God.

We see the same type of range of interpretations when we look at Jewish constructions of Jesus the Jew. For example, we have presentations of Jesus as a Jewish political revolutionary; as a Torah-purist of the rabbinic school of Hillel; as an Essene akin to the community who lived at Qumran and left us the Dead Sea Scrolls; and as a Galilean charismatic leader who was able to work miracles in the name of God.

Each of these views of Jesus is based on the given author's own evaluation of three matters: a) Firstly, the evidence available to us from archaeology and written documents about life in first-century Palestine, especially in the Galilee.

b) Secondly, the evidence available to us in the gospels themselves about Jesus.

c) Finally, and most difficult of all, the most appropriate way in which to bring it all together to produce a coherent picture.

And of course different scholars assess the various materials differently.

Let's take a look at how a few of these *Jewish* scholars have talked about Jesus' life and service to the community of Israel in his own time. In 1973 Geza Vermes wrote what has become one of the most famous and influential books on Jesus this century, entitled, *Jesus the Jew*. He presents Jesus as a *typical* devout sort of prophet figure from the period, and in the following passage compares him to another well-known miracle worker from Rabbinic literature.

> The representation of Jesus in the Gospels as a man whose supernatural abilities derived, not from secret powers, but from immediate contact with God, proves him to be a genuine charismatic, the true heir of an age-old prophetic religious line. But can other contemporary figures be defined in the same way? The answer is yes.

One of the prime characteristics of the ancient
Hasidim or Devout is that their prayer was believed
to be all-powerful, capable of performing miracles.
The best known of these charismatics ... is a first-
century BC saint, called Honi the Circle-Drawer by
the rabbis ...

whereas none of the claims and aspirations of Jesus
can be said definitely to associate him with the role
of Messiah, not to speak of that of son of man ...
everything combines ... to place him in the
venerable company of the Devout, the ancient
Hasidim ... the holy miracle-workers of Galilee.[10]

Vermes seems to have placed Jesus somewhere in
between the traditional Jewish and Christian esti-
mates of his real identity. He does not wish Jesus to
be seen as the Messiah of Israel, and certainly not as
a divine figure, but on the other hand he does view
Jesus as a very significant religious person. Indeed he
goes on to say that when you take Jesus' teachings
into account, then

no objective and enlightened student of the Gospels
can help but be struck by the incomparable
superiority of Jesus ... Second to none in
profundity of insight and grandeur of character, he
is in particular an unsurpassed master of the art of
laying bare the inmost core of spiritual truth and of
bringing every issue back to the essence of religion,
the existential relationship of man and man, and
man and God.[11]

Many Jews will feel that Vermes has gone too far in

his elevation of Jesus as an outstanding Jewish prophet, but we shall return to this issue later. Let us now look at another contemporary Jewish commentator on the life of Jesus. Hyam Maccoby is the librarian at Leo Baeck College in London, a centre for non-Orthodox people who wish a formal training in Jewish teaching and values, etc. In 1973, the same year as Vermes, he published quite a different book entitled, *Revolution In Judaea: Jesus And The Jewish Resistance*. According to Maccoby, Jesus began life as an itinerant prophet-figure, but mid-way through his ministry, when John the Baptist, his fellow-prophet, had been arrested and killed, and when the Messiah whom Jesus prophesied would come had still not appeared, Jesus decided to proclaim himself as the coming Messiah.

> The switch in role from Prophet to King was a dramatic one, unprecedented in Jewish history. Here, if anywhere, the uniqueness of Jesus is to be found …

> The King whom Jesus now announced himself to be was no ordinary king, but the final King-Messiah whose advent was the culmination of human history, the holy King to whom the world would turn as its spiritual head …

> Acclaimed as the rightful King of the Jews, Jesus entered Jerusalem, riding an ass's foal in deliberate fulfilment of the prophecy of Zechariah …

> The Gospel portrayal is hopelessly riddled with contradictions. The simple solution is the obvious one: that Jesus was making a bid for power as a

literal, not metaphorical or 'spiritual,' King of the Jews.[12]

Maccoby has a far less honourable presentation to make of Jesus and of his disciples. He sees Jesus as one of the Jewish resistance leaders who were determined to rid the land of Israel of the Roman occupying power, and to restore it to Jewish sovereignty.

There is no need to see any supernatural power at work in Jesus' life according to this model. Indeed Maccoby goes further and claims that it was Jesus' later followers who created the myth that Jesus was a spiritual King and the founder of a new movement. This picture of Jesus owes much to traditional Jewish reaction to the Jesus movement. Whereas many scholars would want to agree that there was considerable reflection on the person and work of Jesus by those who came after him, there is a general consensus that Maccoby has misread the evidence and so presents a picture of Jesus which is far too cynical, this-worldly, and power-oriented.

We can now look at the assessment of a third Jewish scholar, one who takes a totally different line from the previous two. Harvey Falk, an Orthodox Rabbi in America, wrote a book in 1985 called, *Jesus the Pharisee: A New Look at the Jewishness of Jesus*. In this book he based himself on the teachings of a renowned 18th century Rabbi, Jacob Emden. The view of Jesus the Jew shared by these two rabbis is founded on the notion that he was a faithful Orthodox Jew of his time whose mission in life was to lead *non-Jews* into the spiritual path to salvation which the God of Israel had ordained for them. Falk developed this idea quite considerably, concluding that Jesus in no way intended to start a new direction for Jewish people in their relationship with God.

Jesus, he insisted, had no innovative mission to the Jewish people:

> there seems no question that the Hasid from Nazareth would have objected strenuously to Christian missionary activity among Jews.[13]

What, then, did Jesus have to say that was noteworthy? Falk says that there were essentially two dimensions in Jesus' teaching, one for the Jewish people and one for the non-Jewish world. With respect to the Jewish people, he says that Jesus was a loyal Jew whose interpretation of the Torah and Jewish life was in accordance with one of the two major 'denominations' which were vying for dominance in the Jewish world at the time. The two leading figures were called Hillel and Shammai, the latter of whom was more severe and less welcoming, and whose school of teaching was dominant at the time. Falk sees Jesus as an important spokesman of the former school of teaching, and therefore 'a member of the opposition', as it were:

> Jesus of Nazareth—according to our thesis—never wished to see his fellow Jews change one iota of their traditional faith. He himself remained an Orthodox Jew to his last moment. He only wished to see his people return to the teachings of the School of Hillel, which stressed love, humility, and

the salvation of mankind. His attacks on the
Pharisees were directed against the School of
Shammai, who were in control of the principal
institutions of Judaism in his time.[14]

What then about Jesus' attitude to non-Jews? To
understand Falk's view of this it is necessary first of
all to say a word about what has become the traditional Jewish answer to the question, 'What do non-
Jews have to do to guarantee a place in the world to
come?' Judaism teaches that there is no requirement
for non-Jews to become Jews, and therefore there is
no need for any sort of mission to convert people to
Judaism. Instead, the belief is that God has laid
down a minimum requirement on all of humanity for
a spiritually and morally acceptable life. So long as
people live in accordance with this universal code
they will inherit a place in the world to come.

The belief is that this code of life was given in the
days of Noah, when God made a covenant with the
whole of humanity. First of all, people must be
monotheist, believing in the one Creator God. Secondly, they must accept the so-called Seven Laws of
Noah, which are as follows:

> idolatry is forbidden;
> blasphemy is forbidden;
> murder is forbidden;
> sexual immorality is forbidden;
> theft is forbidden;
> eating from a live animal is forbidden;
> establishing a just legal system is
>   positively commanded.

Falk is convinced that Jesus operated with a version of this same attitude to non-Jews. In fact he reads the gospels as showing that Jesus was a genuine ground-breaker in pioneering this teaching. In effect, Jesus was a missionary to the non-Jewish world, revealing by his teachings and his lifestyle that the God of Israel was indeed the one true God, and that they could have a proper relationship with him, without, however, having to become Jews themselves. Let us now listen to Falk himself:

> Although Judaism never attempted to missionize for converts to its religion ... Moses obligated the Jews to spread knowledge of the Noahide commandments to all mankind...

> the original intent of Jesus ... was to bring the seven Noahide Commandments to the Gentiles, while the Jews should continue their adherence to Judaism...

> the writers of the Gospels never meant to say that the Nazarene came to abolish Judaism, but only that he came to establish a religion for the Gentiles from that time onward. Nor was it new, but actually ancient; they being the Seven Commandments of the Sons of Noah, which were forgotten.[15]

Many readers of Falk's work have pointed out his glaring omission of the fact that Jesus constantly relates salvation and fulfilment in life to a relationship with himself. To read the gospels is to see that it is *not* simply a case of encouraging general good morality among people. Nor does Jesus simply encourage Jews to follow Moses in their service and worship of God, in the way that, say, Amos did, or Rabbi Hillel did. Jesus claimed far more for himself than they ever did.

Therefore it is not a fair reading of the gospels to say that Jesus was simply an advocate for one stream of Pharisaic teaching as opposed to another. It also flies in the face of the evidence to say that Jesus had a mission to non-Jews above all else. Any reading of the gospels highlights passages like the following:

> These twelve Yeshua sent out with the following instructions: 'Don't go into the territory of the Goyim, and don't enter any town in Shomron, but go rather to the lost sheep of the house of Israel.' (Matthew 10:5-6)

> Yeshua left that place and went off to the region of Tzor and Tzidon. A woman from Cana'an who was living there came to him … But Yeshua said … 'I was sent only to the lost sheep of Israel.' (Matthew 15:21, 22, 24)

Passages like these two make it clear that Jesus saw his own mission as essentially to his own people, not to non-Jews. He did, however, give a significant amount of attention to the non-Jewish people whom he encountered, and in the example above from Matthew 15, for instance, he willingly healed the Canaanite woman.

However, non-Jews like her would have realised immediately that if Jesus held the key to fulfilment in their lives, then it was in the context of life lived for the glory of the God of *Israel*, and for no other. And Jewish people would themselves have been left in no doubt that Jesus' self-understanding only made sense in the context of the various 'Messianic' promises in their Scriptures. Both Jews and non-Jews would have sensed the 'extra dimension' of Jesus' life and teaching.

We are back at the central issue of how to affirm the genuineness and indispensability of Jesus' Jewishness without in any way reducing him to being simply a man of his generation.

Here, then, are three different views of Jesus the Jew from the pens of three different Jewish scholars. Each of these reconstructions has its limitations and its presuppositions, but at the same time each has also contributed to the refining of the picture of Jesus which emerges from the gospels. In spite of the lack of agreement among the various schools of thought, Christian scholars, on the whole, are convinced that the contribution of Jewish scholarship and expertise with respect to the time of Jesus' life is proving to be invaluable in re-discovering the historical Jesus.

The title of this chapter is a partial quotation from the turn of the century, when a German non-Jewish scholar, Julius Wellhausen wrote a statement which deeply affected both the Church and the Synagogue. In his book on the first three gospels, he stated:

Jesus was not a Christian, but a Jew.[16]

These words have driven and haunted Jesus research

ever since. Never again could the Jewishness of Jesus be ignored or undervalued. Because there is a great deal of truth in these words, it is clear that Jewish insights must play their part alongside those of Christians in allowing Jesus to fully be himself in every generation and culture. Of course there have been strong negative reactions to Wellhausen's claim by non-Jews, notably in Nazi-influenced theology. But this in itself shows how deeply the debate was engaging the Churches. Nazis were frightened that this exploration into the Jewishness of Jesus might lead to a positive attitude towards Jewishness more generally.

As it turns out, the Jewishness of Jesus is at last beginning to feature more prominently in many contemporary documents being published by Church authorities. For example, there is the considerable progress in Roman Catholic attitudes and documents. We can see this as we follow attitudes from the famous 1965 Vatican Two Council, through to the publication of the 1985 'Notes on the Correct Way to Present the Jews and Judaism in Preaching and Catechesis in the Roman Catholic Church'. Section Three of these Notes is devoted to the 'Jewish Roots of Christianity', and it opens with words which are, in their own way, as unexpected and significant as were Wellhausen's some eighty years earlier:

Jesus was, and always remained, a Jew.

So then, rediscovering the Jewishness of Jesus is an adventure waiting for both Jews and Christians. One difference, of course, is that Christians are coming from a lifetime of reading the gospels and talking about Jesus, whereas Jewish people are coming to Jesus more or less from the cold. A marvellously enriching, but also challenging, experience awaits the Jewish person who is prepared to listen to Jesus for himself/herself.

6.

Yesterday's Jewish Responses To Jesus

I n spite of all that has been said so far, the response of many Jewish people is still to resort to the traditional views of Jesus as a deceiver and a blasphemer. Here are some more quotes from actual conversations with Jewish people:

> 'Look, it might be true that Jesus started off as a good Jew, but after a while he got caught up in a lot of other stuff, and just went wrong somehow. He lost sight of real Judaism.'

> 'We've had plenty of false messiahs in Judaism, and they all seemed genuine to the Jews who followed them. Some of them knew what they were doing, and were trying to exploit us, though some were probably convinced in their own minds that they were God's man. And that's a kind of sickness. Now I don't know where Jesus fits in there, though I'm prepared to give him the benefit of the doubt and say that he was in the grip of a religious mania,

rather than being someone who was a power-seeker.'

'My rabbi told me once that Jesus came from an immoral family and that he grew up an immoral man. He tried to use religion to get him what he wanted out of life; he had forbidden relationships with different women, especially Mary Magdalen; and he committed blasphemy without any shame. He brought shame and disgrace to the Jewish community!'

These kinds of attitudes which are shown in the 1990s, by Orthodox communities in particular, are the very ones which were laid down from the 4th century on. All religious communities have a tendency to be conservative, and to change their attitudes only with reluctance, and so we find a great resistance to looking at Jesus in a new light among large numbers of Jewish people. What I think would be useful at this point is to present an outline of these traditional Jewish views of Jesus. It will be familiar to some readers, but may prove to be of help to others.

There is hardly any actual reference to Jesus in the rabbinic literature of the period when the Talmud was being compiled, which is to say until the close of the first six centuries of the Common Era. At the close of this period not only was the Talmud established as the constitution, so to speak, of the Jewish people, but the Jewish community as a whole had come through a long process of struggle to find a confident self-definition.

This was, in short, the time of the formation of

what we have come to know as the Jewish identity. So there is some significance in the fact that there is no real place for Jesus in the sacred texts of that period.

Some interpret this silence about Jesus to mean that not only was he not important to the formation of Judaism, he wasn't even important enough to mention as a figure in Israel's history.

However, there can be no real doubt about the significance of Jesus for the actual history of the Jewish people during that period. This was the formative period when both the Jewish and the Christian communities were absorbed in establishing their boundaries and definitions. In particular, each community was conscious of the claims of the other, and therefore much of each community's self-definition took place in the context of the self-definition of the *other* community. Jews and Christians alike were at pains to show that they alone had the right interpretations and applications of the Scripture and of God's work in history.

Because issues like the correct way to interpret the Hebrew Bible, the correct way to understand history, and the correct way to discern God's redeeming hand in Israel's own history were very much to the fore Jesus' own claims about himself, and also those made on his behalf by his followers, must certainly have been on the Jewish agenda. Why then, if there had been some considerable discussion about Jesus in rabbinic conversations and sermons, should there be no reference to him in the rabbinic *literature* of the time?

Well, neither community would wish to advertise the 'successes' of the other, so of course the Jewish leaders would certainly not have wished to draw attention to Jesus in their own teaching material at the same time as they were trying to prevent their people from considering him and his claims. The rabbis were determined to isolate their community from any consideration of his teachings or life, and from any contact with his followers, especially *Jewish* people who believed that Jesus was the Messiah.

It is entirely probable that the lack of reference to Jesus and to the birth and growth of the early communities of Jewish followers of Jesus was the result of a conscious decision by the rabbinic authorities to avoid, and indeed prevent, discussions of Jesus in the Jewish community.

What is more, what little mention there is of Jesus, or even of those Jewish people who became his followers, comes from the period of the 3rd to 5th centuries of the Christian Era rather than that of the 1st and 2nd centuries. In other words, there are no accounts of, or remarks about, Jesus from religious leaders of Jesus' own generation. This means that the gospels are the only *first*-century documents which give us accounts of the Jewishness of Jesus and of early Jewish reactions to him.

Once again we note that reactions to Jesus are, as often as not, based on reactions to his followers. The Talmudic literature was written generations after Jesus, and comes out of the context of mutual confrontation between the emerging Christian and Jewish communities.

When Jesus *is* spoken of in the Rabbinic literature, he is regularly referred to as 'that man/so-and-so', or, by some form of symbolic name. Here is a typical example of such a reference:

> Rabbi Simeon ben Azzai said: I found a family register in Jerusalem and in it was written, 'So-and-so' is a bastard through a transgression of the law concerning 'your neighbour's wife'.[17]

This is a thinly veiled reference to the fact that Jesus' mother and father, Mary and Joseph, had not been married when Jesus was conceived. Christians see this as a miraculous virgin birth, in fulfilment of a famous prophecy in Isaiah 7:14 ('a virgin will conceive'), but obviously the Jewish authorities interpreted it as proof of pre-marital sexual relations. In the following quote we see a reference to Jesus under another name, this time in the context of a debate about the proper death penalty for Jewish people who try to lead other Jewish people into idolatry. The consensus is that the death penalty is definitely appropriate, and then these words are found:

> And thus they did to 'Ben Stada' in Lydda, and they hung him on the eve of Passover.[18]

'Ben Stada' is one of the names found in rabbinic literature for Jesus. What we have in this passage is an allusion to the crucifixion of Jesus at Passover time, as we read it in the gospels.

The English name, 'Jesus', is simply a version of his actual Hebrew name, which would have been

'Yeshua' (essentially the same name as Joshua). This name is formed from a Hebrew root which has to do with 'salvation', so that Yeshua was the one who was to be the 'saviour' of Israel. By playing with this name, the rabbis occasionally called him 'Yeshu', a variation in spelling and pronunciation. Here is a characteristic example of this:

On the eve of the Passover, Yeshu was hanged.[19]

The significance of this last name is that it soon came to be used as an acronym by his opponents. An acronym is a word which might actually be a word, or maybe a title, or some such thing, but whose letters are used to form the initials for another whole set of words. These other words then provide a message of some sort which is supposed to relate to the original word or title.

In this case, the letters which spell out 'Yeshu', the way that the rabbis wrote Jesus' name, namely Y SH U, were used to spell out a Hebrew curse,

'Yimach

Shemo

Uzzikhrono'.

This means, 'May his name and memory be blotted out'. In other words, even if originally the two names Yeshu and Yeshua were quite interchangeable, as some think, the tradition soon arose that 'Yeshu' was to be preferred, since it allowed the speaker to communicate a curse without actually saying the words! To this day, many Orthodox Jewish people keep this tradition alive. I myself have heard a grandfather explaining it in this way to his grandson.

Two important points are worth making about the presentation of Jesus in these texts. First of all, there is no denial that Jesus actually was an historical person, though there is some confusion about the exact dates of his life. They were all too close in time to the events of Jesus' life to be able to deny his existence, and, of course, there would still have been a lot of talk about him in spite of the attempts by the authorities to silence this. It is one thing to present someone whom you perceive as an enemy in a bad light, but it is altogether more difficult to deny that he/she even existed.

Nonetheless it is true to say that if all we had was the evidence of the rabbinic literature then we would never know just how exercised the Jewish leadership was by the impact of the Jesus movement within the Jewish community. To put it another way, if we take a longer view of history, this strategy of deliberate silence about Jesus did prove to be successful, in the sense that by the dawn of the modern era in history, discussion of Jesus by the Jewish community, and awareness of his Jewishness, had all but disappeared.

Secondly, the picture which is given of Jesus is one in which he is denigrated as a blasphemer and heretic who went so far as to exploit the divine Name in order to get power for himself and lead the Jewish people away from their true path of faithfulness to God. In step with this portrait of a spiritual deceiver is the added portrayal of Jesus as a grossly immoral man. What we have here is not an attempt at an accurate historical biography, but a piece of propaganda aimed at isolating Jesus from the Jewish community. A few more examples will suffice to get a feel of the kind of material. In this first one, a rabbi is commenting upon a word of Balaam, a false prophet, found in the Bible, in Numbers 24:23. He uses it as an opportunity to criticize Jesus' claim that he would be resurrected from the dead by the power of God:

> Rabbi Simeon ben Lakish said: 'Woe to him who makes himself alive by the name of God.'[20]

This is understood by the rabbis as meaning that Jesus was guilty of blasphemy, in thinking that he could manipulate God into doing miracles for him. We have already mentioned a passage in the Talmud where Jesus is referred to by the name 'Yeshu', and that passage goes on to say that before Jesus was executed

> a herald went forth and cried: 'He is going forth to be [executed] because he has practised sorcery and enticed Israel to apostasy. Any one who can say anything in his favour, let him come forward and plead on his behalf.' But since nothing was brought forward in his favour he was hanged on the eve of the Passover.[21]

To summarise, then, at this point: when Judaism's foundational sacred literature was being created, references to Jesus and those Jewish people who followed him were kept to a bare minimum.

What was allowed to be reported was in the

nature of attacks on Jesus' spiritual and moral integrity. This picture remained the dominant one in the Jewish community.

Perhaps this would be an opportune place to examine another significant passage in the gospels, one which reflects something of this antagonism to Jesus *and to his followers* in the days of the beginning of the Jesus movement, if we may call it that. We know that in about year 80 of the Common Era the rabbinic leadership of the Jewish people in Palestine commissioned a special prayer to be included in the daily prayer service which would make it virtually impossible for Jewish believers in Jesus to remain within the synagogue community.

There is a basic set of prayers to this day, called the Shemoneh Esrei, which means 'The Eighteen', whose origin goes back to the time of Jesus, if not earlier in parts. These prayers form the backbone of the synagogue service. Now although they are still known by this name, The Eighteen, there are actually nineteen of them. The nineteenth is this extra prayer which was composed to deter or perhaps exclude Jewish believers in Jesus. It is quite likely that other Jewish people who were considered to be 'heretics' were also intended in this prayer, but it certainly included Jewish believers in Jesus.

Most modern versions of this prayer to be found in Jewish Prayer Books have toned down the language somewhat, but an early version of it, found in a storeroom in Cairo has the following form:

For the apostates let there be no hope, and may the

arrogant kingdom soon be rooted out in our days,
and the Nazarenes and the sectarians perish as in a
moment and be blotted out from the Book of Life,
and with the righteous may they not be inscribed.
Blessed are You, O Lord, who humbles the
arrogant.[22]

The prayer was presumably intended to either dis-
suade these Jewish believers (and others) from
attending synagogue services, since they could
hardly recite this prayer against themselves and their
families, or to help identify any such Jewish believers
who were until that time unknown in a synagogue,
since they would tend to be silent during the chan-
ting of the prayer. The overall purpose was to
remove these peoople from the synagogue. What has
to be kept in mind is that we are not speaking of a
culture and community like today's typical western
city, where there is a large choice of places of worship
to attend. In the Jewish communities of the world in
those times the synagogue was the centre of all social
life. To be put out of the synagogue meant to be
excommunicated from the Jewish community.
Indeed up until very modern times this continued to
be the case for Jewish people within their communities.

What is certain is that the composition of a specific prayer in 80 C.E. did not emerge from an historical vacuum. Before that would have happened there
would have been a period of growing suspicion and
antagonism, and without doubt plenty of cases of
Jewish followers of Jesus being put out of the community. The prayer, in other words, would have

been the climax of a process of alienation rather than its first step. And so we can now turn to the ninth chapter of John's gospel, where we see something of the early stages of this growing antagonism towards the Jesus movement.

The chapter opens with Jesus healing a man who had been born blind. Equally important is the fact that this healing took place on the Sabbath. Jewish law held that healing should not be done on the Sabbath since it violated the injunction not to work on the Sabbath. If it was a case of possible life or death then it was different, and doing whatever was necessary to save a person was positively commanded. But if the healing could be left until after the Sabbath, then it should be. Of course this miraculous healing caused astonishment among the people who knew the man, and word spread throughout the whole Jewish community. In time some of the Pharisees heard of it, and some of them at least were not happy:

> The man who had been born blind was brought before the Pharisees. As it was a sabbath day when Jesus made the paste and opened his eyes, the Pharisees too asked him how he had gained his sight.

When the man tells them the bare details, there is a mixed reaction among the Pharisees to what they are hearing about Jesus:

> Some of the Pharisees said, 'This man cannot be from God; he does not keep the sabbath.' Others

said, 'How could such signs come from a sinful man?'

Things get quite heated and some of them actually doubt that the man was ever blind. In other words they suspect that Jesus does not have the power to heal, and that either Jesus and the man had conspired to produce a 'miracle' for some self-serving purpose, or that the man himself had seen Jesus' presence as a way to enter the seeing world after his years of pretending to be blind.

It is to be remembered that to this very day the existence of 'professional beggars' in some societies is well known and actually condoned. These people also have to make a living! So the Pharisees visit the man's parents to check on him.

'Is this your son? Do you say that he was born blind? How is it that he can see now?' The parents replied, 'We know that he is our son, and that he was born blind. But how it is that he can now see, or who opened his eyes, we do not know. Ask him; he is of age; let him speak for himself.'

Why this callous attitude? Perhaps his parents themselves were too shocked to be able to support their son, and so also wanted to hear him tell his story again? Perhaps they were opposed to the ministry of Jesus themselves, and so disapproved of what their son had got involved with? The text itself provides an answer:

His parents gave this answer because they were

afraid ... for the Jewish authorities had already agreed that anyone who acknowledged Jesus as Messiah should be banned from the synagogue. That is why the parents said, 'He is of age; ask him.'

There we have it, then. His parents are afraid that if they defend their son, this will be interpreted as supporting Jesus, and will therefore lead to their religious and social ostracism.

This cost is too high for them. As the controversy continues, the man himself grows more confident, and he concludes by defending Jesus and challenging the authority and integrity of those who are attacking Jesus. What his parents feared for themselves happens to him. The text simply says that they 'turned him out'.

This is a classic example of a situation which has been repeated countless times since. Even today, a large percentage of Jewish people who believe that Jesus is the Messiah will tell a similar story of how their families and friends turned them out when they learned of their faith. In the more serious cases, such Jewish believers will have their names struck out of family or community records, and their names will never be mentioned again. This is not just a mark of rejection of their faith, but also serves as part of the community's strategy of dissuading others from following suit. Jesus and all who follow him are presented in such a bad light that it enters the realm of slander and complete misrepresentation.

As I said above, when Judaism's foundational sacred literature was being created, references to

Jesus and those Jewish people who followed him were kept to a bare minimum. What was said lay in the nature of attacks on the spiritual and moral integrity of Jesus and his followers.

By the ninth century, a whole series of insults against Jesus had long been created and widely circulated. Indeed they were now being crystallized into various versions of a popular piece of literature which came to be known as *Toldot Yeshu*, the 'History/Generations of Jesus'. This work claims to be an account of the life of Jesus, but in content, tone, and intention it is clearly just a piece of propaganda. It was aimed not only at showing that Jesus was a blasphemer and a sorcerer, but also at ridiculing him as a Jew who should have known better, but who nevertheless went hopelessly and horribly wrong. Its purpose was clearly to provide such a scurrilous picture of Jesus that it would drastically reduce the possibility of any Jewish person seriously considering the claims of the real Jesus. In truth it does not even make a good show of giving an accurate historical account of the life of Jesus.

Some of the stories which made up this tradition about Jesus have been translated into English, and I will give two of them here as examples of the anti-Jesus material being gathered and published in the Jewish community at the start of the medieval period.

> Now it was a custom of the disciples of the wise that neither youth nor lad should pass by the way without his head being covered and his eyes toward the ground out of the respect of disciples for their

masters. But on a certain day that wicked one [sic!] passed by while the rabbis were seated in a body at the gate of the synagogue ...

... that wicked one did pass by in front of our masters with erect stature and uncovered head, saluting no one, but with shameless forehead exposing himself to his master.[23]

Jesus is being presented as arrogant and in contempt of the Jewish community even as a young lad. This arrogance is said to have grown as he himself grew older. When he was a young adult he is held to have sought the forbidden power which would give him the authority over others which he felt was his by right:

in the temple was the foundation-stone ... and on it were graven the letters of the Ineffable Name. And whosoever learned them could do whatsoever he would...

Dogs of brass were bound to two pillars of iron at the gate of the place of burnt-offerings, so that whosoever entered and learnt the letters, as soon as he went forth the dogs bayed at him: if he then looked at them the letters went forth from his mind.

Then came Jesus and learned them, and wrote upon parchment and cut open his thigh and laid the parchment with those letters therein; so that the cutting of his flesh pained him not. And he restored the flesh to its place. And as he went forth the dogs of the pillars bayed at him, and the letters went forth from his mind. He went into his house, and cut into his flesh with a knife, and lifted out the writing and learnt the letters.

Then he went forth and gathered together three hundred and ten of the young men of Israel. He saith unto them … I am the Messiah, and them that withstand me are the children of whoredoms …[24]

This is a most important passage for the opponents of Jesus, as it is seeking to·account for his ability to perform miracles. It is to be noted that there was no attempt made to deny Jesus' power, only to claim that he gained that power by committing several grave sins. His relationship with God is said to be not that of a loving, obedient son, as shown in the gospels, but that of a deceiving charlatan, out only to exploit the power of God for his own purposes.

Jewish scholars today consistently maintain that Toldot Yeshu has no historical value whatsoever for the life of Jesus. But it does of course have immense importance for our study of the attitudes of Jewish communities to Jesus and the Church, and in particular to Jewish believers in the Church. Toldot Yeshu became the prime, if not the sole, source of the Jewish community's information about Jesus from the early Middle Ages to the early 20th century in Eastern Europe. The various accounts are made up of stories of Jesus' illegitimacy, blasphemy, immorality and thirst for power.

They all present him as a thoroughly wicked Jewish man, one of whom the Jewish community should be ashamed, and at whose actions and attitudes it should be outraged.

If you like, these stories were an early form of Jewish tract, to be passed on by word of mouth as well as in written form. They served to give the Jewish people the image of Jesus which their religious leaders wished them to have. And of course relationships with the Church were so terrible at this same time that it was very difficult indeed for any Jewish person to get a true indication of who Jesus really was! Using Jesus' own words that you can know what someone is really like by examining the fruit of her/his life, Jewish people took their experiences of typical Christian behaviour towards them as proof that the stories about Jesus' *own* wickedness and obsession with power were true.

In fact I am quite sure that another way in which these tracts served the Jewish people was in giving them a means to fight back against Christian anti-semitism. What could the community do? What could any individual Jewish person do? They had neither power in society nor recourse to fair treatment. Recrimination and retaliation against any perceived Jewish challenge to Christian supremacy was swift and severe. And so the Jewish community would do the only thing which it could: it would gather together and laugh at the beliefs of the Christians by ridiculing and condemning their founder.

There was one other important source of information about Jesus for the Jewish community in the Middle Ages, but it was equally negative, though in a different way. The Church, intent on convincing

Jewish people that Jesus was the Messiah, but lacking any real spirit of dialogue, began to see religious capital in *imposing* formal controversies on the Jewish communities of Europe. These so-called 'Disputations' were structured like an open dialogue between Christian theologians (quite often 'converts' from Judaism) and Jewish religious leaders.

But in reality the Jewish participants were placed in a situation in which it was impossible for them to 'win' the disputation.

What took place was, of course, simply an exercise in trying to score points against the other person and his community. The Jewishness of Jesus was not on the Christian agenda, for all that they spoke of him as the one who fulfilled all things Jewish.

What was on the agenda was debate about the proper interpretation of Messianic passages in the Hebrew Bible; debate about the true nature of God, especially with respect to the concept of the Trinity; debate about whether or not rabbinic writings and Jewish mystical texts contained proofs of the Messiahship of Jesus; and debate about the correct interpretation of history since the time of Jesus, specifically the desolation of Jewry in contrast to the triumph of Christendom.

The Jewish spokesmen knew that it might be better anyway for the Jewish community were they to 'lose' the debate, and so they often backed away from any real discussion of the issues. The truth of the matter is that when such a Disputation took place and the Christian 'won', then there was often a surge of activity to put pressure on the whole Jewish community to accept defeat and 'convert' to Christianity. On the other hand, should the *Jewish* leader presume to 'win', then there was usually a bitter reaction on behalf of many clergy and people who wished to punish the Jews for daring to shame the Church. In either case, it was a no-win situation for the Jewish community, which soon learned to fear these open disputes about Jesus. There was little authentic debate from the Christians, who were out to score points against the Jews; and there was little direct talk from the Jews, who feared the consequences if they spoke at their most eloquent and passionate.

What we find, in short, is that the Jewish leaders were most concerned about protecting their people, not discussing the finer points of doctrine. This type of public debate therefore did nothing for the development of real Jesus research. It either helped to further a hostile attitude to Jesus, or, at best, led to a 'cold neutrality', as someone has called it.

One can therefore sum up the attitude to Jesus which resulted from the interaction between Christians and Jews in the period before the modern era quite easily. Because of the antisemitism of the Church, expressed in contemptuous attitudes, social alienation, theological triumphalism and outright persecution, Jewish people came to fear and hate Jesus and everything to do with him.

And on the other hand, because of the reaction by Jewish leaders to this antisemitism and anti-Judaism, Jewish people were subject to an inner-Jewish portrait of Jesus which was guaranteed to make him an object of moral disgrace and spiritual outrage.

Therefore there were two dynamics at work in what has become the traditional rejection of Jesus. Not only did Jewish people experience a reaction away from Jesus due to the attitudes and behaviour of the Church, but they were also subject to a well-organised counter-interpretation of life by the rabbis, who developed their own theological system for interpreting the life and work of Jesus of Nazareth. As a result of all this, Jewish people did not consider Jesus a worthy subject of discussion, nor did they feel the need to take his words seriously.

This situation remained the case right up till the dawn of the modern era in history. To the Church's shame, Jewish people could not look *out*, as it were, to see Jesus, because the Church was in the way. Equally, Jewish people could not look *inwards* to their own sources to see him, since those sources were deliberately biased against him.

Things began to change, though, with the coming of the modern period, and it is time to see why.

7

The Dawn Of The Modern Era

Without doubt, the two key events in the modern Jewish reconsideration of Jesus were the very events which forever changed the state of modern Jewry in *every* area of its life, namely the *Jewish Enlightenment* (following on from the general European Enlightenment) and the *Jewish Emancipation*. The 18th and 19th centuries saw the gradual opening of western society to Jewish involvement and participation, and although this was a cause of rejoicing in some quarters, Jewish religious leaders saw it as a terrible threat to Jewish survival. In particular they feared a drastic change of attitude to the traditional Jewish values and ways. Attitudes to Jesus were part of the great changes which did, in fact, occur.

The 'Enlightenment' is the name given to the intellectual movement which transformed western society with a series of inter-linked challenges to the status quo. This movement challenged the Church's monopoly of authority in society; it went so far as to challenge the very concept of revelation or absolute knowledge at all; its leaders insisted that human reason was the proper tool for establishing a mature civilisation; they maintained that human beings had within themselves the ability to achieve knowledge about humanity and the universe. They stressed the supremacy of experimental science, by which the laboratory testing of facts and theories became a metaphor for the testing of all truth claims. The Enlightenment marked the aggressive progress of a belief in humankind as a self-endorsing, creative, and capable life-form of great ability and even greater potential.

A major aspect of this movement involved a commitment to the separation of Church and State in society. Its supporters were striving forwards to what they claimed to be the 'light' of modern, liberal and rational thought, leaving behind them the 'darkness' of the past, shackled as it was by religious superstition, arrogance and ritual. Leaders of the Enlightenment were therefore determined to remove any kind of dogma from the basic values and structures of society. People should no longer have to accept religious dogmas of any sort to be full members of any modern society. Religious minorities were to be accorded full protection and freedom of expression. This, of course, was met with great enthusiasm by many Jewish people.

In the Jewish community, as in the rest of Europe, there was also found an increased questioning by many people of all accepted authority and tradition.

Jewish people were also increasingly attracted to faith in the supremacy of reason over dogma and mystery; to commitment to open enquiry and experiment; to a determination to foster religious tolerance; to the priority of morality over theology; and to a commitment to the separation of Church and State which would involve the separation of Synagogue and membership of the Jewish community as well. Why, they argued, should a Jewish person have to be an Orthodox Jew in belief and practice to be considered really Jewish?

The leaders of the Jewish Enlightenment were convinced that a major reason Jews were persecuted was because they persevered in living in the dark past, a past which society around them rightly considered obsolete and crude. Jews were too different from the non-Jewish world in terms of their culture, language, educational policy, ritual observance, etc. 'Enlightened' Jews were therefore determined to eradicate the traditional dogmas and practices of Jewry. It can be clearly seen, therefore, that the possibility was also now there for Jewish people to re-think the traditional attitude to Jesus.

When we speak of the 'Emancipation' of the Jews, what we are referring to is the gradual abolition of the disqualifications and unjust treatments which had been meted out specifically to the Jewish people by European society. We are also referring to the positive granting of religious, civil, and political rights to Jewish (as to other) people for the first time. Jewish people no longer had to live in ghettoes, or be restricted to certain professions, or live in a country simply at the discretion of its leadership. In some areas the changes were indeed quite radical: citizenship was granted to Jewish people, and admission was given to politics, higher education and the arts, etc. Nothing was ever to be the same again in any sphere of Jewish intellectual, social or religious life. All of this also had an impact on attitudes to *Jesus* within the Jewish community.

This change in attitudes to Jesus was expressed by one of the most significant rabbis in the USA, Rabbi Stephen S.Wise, at a public meeting in New York in 1925. He said the following about the translation into English that year of Joseph Klausner's sympathetic book on Jesus:

> It marks the first chapter in a new literature. Such a book could never have been written years ago … Thank God the time has come when men are allowed to be frank, sincere and truthful in their beliefs.[25]

The context for this new attitude was the momentum of political freedom in which Jewish people were able to develop confidence in speaking *publicly* about Jesus at all. This relative freedom for Jewish people to express opinions about Jesus was made possible above all by the fact that there was developing a general social and cultural context in which even the traditional Christian views of Jesus were being challenged in the wider *Christian* community itself. Because new ideas about the person and work of Jesus were being accorded respect in the new liberal Christian environment, Jewish perspectives were cautiously sought as well, by people trying to discover what such an old/new Jesus would look like.

Up until the late 18th century, Jews and Christians only really encountered each other as adversaries. The whole relationship was under the domination and control of the theological dogmas which formed the basis of how each community defined itself vis-à-vis the other. The Enlightenment, and perhaps most especially the rise of historical scepticism in the 19th century, made it possible for the new liberally-minded Jews and Christians to ignore dogma, whether about Christ or Torah. Dogma no longer defined the boundaries. Jews and Christians began to examine one another's faith, ethics, and community life more openly and with considerable curiosity.

Liberal Christians began to look at Jesus in a new, non-Orthodox light. Liberal Jews, already living in a manner no longer dominated by the Torah as defined by the Orthodox rabbis, began to question whether such a new-look Jesus could be a suitable person for Jewish people to investigate as well. Of course one must not forget that antisemitism was still alive and well throughout this entire period. There was no desire among liberal Christian scholars to bring about a full social reconciliation with the Jewish people. Judaism was still denigrated as legalistic, in contrast to Jesus' gracious ethics of love.

Jewish spokesmen were well aware of the continuing negative attitude towards them, but nonetheless they began to take the opportunity being given to them to speak more openly about Jesus. In fact one outcome of this complex situation was that some Jewish intellectuals began to differentiate more and more boldly between the Christian Church which they lived with every day of their lives, and Jesus himself. This educated intuition that there was more to Jesus than met the eye in the life of the churches began to spread, and many were beginning to think positively of Jesus as 'the teacher from Nazareth'.

The world of scholarship came increasingly under the influence of rationalism, specifically the rationalising of religion, whereby it was held that if religious and moral ideals were to be considered at all valid in the modern and enlightened world, then they had to be of *universal* significance. Jesus was therefore being increasingly presented as the very model of the universal ethical ideals of every civilized, rational society. At the same time, Jewish scholars were presenting these very same ethical ideals as lying at the heart of Judaism. And so Jesus, in a radical departure from the closed ways of the past, was held up as the model of Jewish—and universal—morality and spirituality. These 'liberal' scholars were determined to be emancipated from what they saw as the prisons of their respective orthodox traditions, and both groups wanted to emancipate Jesus from the dogma of the traditional Jewish and Christian perspectives.

Martin Buber, in his 1930 book, *Two Types of Faith*, showed a strong desire to see this development continue. David Novak, the Professor of Modern Jewish Thought at the University of Virginia summed up Buber's position very well:

> Buber wants to release Jesus from the confines of
> both Christian and Jewish dogma. The former
> makes too much of him, and the latter too little.[26]

Liberal Christians will applaud Buber's evaluation,
agreeing that too much has been made of Jesus by
Christians down the centuries, but of course they
share many of the same presuppositions as Buber.
Orthodox Christian believers will object, however,
that one *cannot* make too much of Jesus. They view
this whole exercise as nothing more than a successful
attempt to escape from the real challenge of Jesus by
re-creating him in this group of people's own image.
Nevertheless, this was the situation that developed
throughout the 19th century.

At the turn of the present century, then, many
Jewish people were learning that they could escape
the caricature of Jesus as a deluded, blasphemous
and illegitimate person. And many Christians of different types were realising the error of seeing Jesus as
either not really Jewish at all, or else as so unique
that he had nothing in common with other Jews.

It is important to emphasize that this movement
towards a new appreciation of Jesus in the Jewish
community has only involved those Jewish people
who are true children of the Enlightenment and the
Emancipation. The traditional, Orthodox communities, as a rule, resisted this change, and continue to
resist it. To this day they generally continue to oper-
ate on the level of avoiding all conversation about
'that man' of the Talmud. When he is mentioned, it
is to describe him in terms of the same stereotypes

which were developed in the early centuries of the growth of the Jesus movement.

In large measure this is part of their reaction against what they see as the widespread secularization of the Jewish people in the modern period. It is actually a part of their overall negative response to the *Enlightenment*, with its drive for the supremacy of free enquiry, reason, and the search for universal ideals. It is therefore not necessarily a specific reaction against the purported Jewishness of Jesus. Relatively few Orthodox Jews are involved in the search to rediscover the Jewishness of Jesus, and those individuals who are involved do not really represent mainstream Orthodoxy.

Of course it must also be emphasized that the so-called 'Reform Jews' of the 18th and 19th centuries were essentially setting out to challenge their own community's traditional understanding of itself and its role in the modern world. So their investigation of Jesus must actually be understood as part of the quest for *Jewish* self-identity. These Jewish thinkers were not concerned with helping Christians to develop their Christian faith. They were working to develop a Judaism without dogma, a faith for their own community which was freed, as they felt it should be, from old rituals and from what they considered to be an unhealthy belief in the supernatural.

They also wanted a lifestyle and a relationship model which was liberated from the domination of *halakhah*, which is the traditional system of Jewish law. Jesus was therefore viewed primarily (once he had been freed from Christian dogma) as a most important representative of the universal ethic of Judaism (once it too had been set free from dogma).

Bernard Felsenthal, a leading Reform rabbi in America in the second half of the 19th century, was caught up in the reclamation of Jesus for the Jewish community to such an extent that he once said the following:

> The religion of Christ is essentially identical with the religion of Israel. Paradoxical as it may sound, it is nevertheless true that the Jews are the true Christians, and that the so-called Christians are not Christians, inasmuch as they profess a number of doctrines totally foreign to the religion of Christ.[27]

Here we have a Jewish person telling Christians what they may legitimately believe about Jesus! Quite a reversal of the usual roles, and only really possible in the USA of those times, committed as it was to real religious pluralism. Take the dogma out, he says, and Jews and Christians can come together. In a 1901 book written by the American Reform rabbi, Joseph Krauskopf, the following words are to be found, words which capture exactly the motivating agenda of that particular Jewish approach to Jesus:

> when the Jew shall have completely cast away his obstructive exclusiveness and ceremonialism, and the Christian his Christology, Jew and Gentile will be one.[28]

Most of this Jewish optimism and enthusiasm about

a new relationship between Jews and Christians, including a fresh appreciation of Jesus the Jew, was shattered during the pogroms in Russia in the 1880s, and then also during the Hitler years in Europe. Once again terrible experiences at the hands of churches and church members were to provide the most influential picture of Jesus for the Jewish community. We must never lose sight of this fact, and Christians need to realize that they themselves bear the largest part of the responsibility for the Jewish antagonism to Jesus.

That isn't quite the whole story, of course, since the Jewish community's leadership also has its own interest in keeping Jesus off the agenda.

Nonetheless, the overall momentum within the Jewish community, which began with the Enlightenment and Emancipation, to somehow get back to Jesus himself, has never been lost. The present Jewish generation is perhaps able again to play a large part in renewing this momentum. In the next chapter we will examine what is happening in *contemporary* Jewish scholarship on 'Jesus ben Joseph, the Jew from Nazareth'.

8

Today's Jewish Responses To Jesus

What exactly is happening today then? The Jewish community still takes a strong stand against Jesus being the Messiah promised to Israel by God. Most leaders of the Jewish community still condemn and denigrate those Jewish people who have come to believe that Jesus is, in fact, the Messiah of Israel.

But on the other hand, scholars in the community have overcome one major handicap which faces the average Jewish person: the handicap which says that it is forbidden for a Jewish person to so much as read a gospel or listen to the words of Jesus. Schools and higher education institutions in Israel, as well as certain Jewish colleges throughout the western world, are looking at the New Testament as a legitimate source of Jewish knowledge. Jesus is being brought back into Jewish history. There is widespread confidence that Jesus of Nazareth, the Jewish man of Galilee, can be discovered. Jews are becoming convinced that they can bring a needed realism to the human picture of Jesus.

Of course the attempt to present Jesus as a Jew takes different forms. Some Jewish leaders are primarily interested in getting a realistic picture of Jesus, whom they see as an important person from first-century Palestine. Already in 1888 a leading American Reform rabbi, Isaac Mayer Wise, was dismissing in no uncertain terms what he saw as unacceptably over-spiritualized Christian presentations of Jesus. Such

> lives of Christ or biographies of Jesus are works of fiction, erected by imagination on the shifting foundation of meagre and unreliable records.[29]

Wise was simply convinced that only an unbiased Jew could be at all trusted to present an undistorted picture of Jesus. But of course this was just another form of vested interest, since there is no such thing as an unbiased person when it comes to the issue of deciding who Jesus really is. Wise, for his part, was prejudging that belief in a supernatural God who intervenes in history on behalf of his people was unacceptable in a modern context. As well as this, he was also convinced that Jesus was not the Messiah, whether using Christian or Jewish definitions of the term. Wise's presupposition was that his type of presentation of Jesus would reveal all that there was to be known about him.

But that, of course, was, and remains, the very point at issue.

Taking a different line altogether, there are several Orthodox rabbis around today who are so determined to prove that Jesus is not the Messiah, that they have chosen to keep alive the old prejudiced stories and presentations about Jesus which we looked at in a previous chapter. These attitudes and activities are hugely discredited by responsible Jewish spokespersons, but many Jewish people today are being exposed to this jaundiced view of Jesus, and so it is important to give an example of the sort of thing which is being said. The following comes from the pen of a widely-read and influential American, Samuel Levine:

> If it is wrong to resist evil, would it be wrong to shoot a potential murderer or rapist? Would you shoot someone who is about to rape your mother or wife? Jesus said ... 'resist not evil, but whosoever shall smite thee on thy right cheek, turn to him the other also.'
>
> Furthermore, a good Christian would agree that if a burglar came and was caught robbing you of your jewelry, you should not punish him or judge him, since that would be a violation of the above verse as well as the mandate of ... 'Judge not, that ye be not judged.'
>
> The New Testament itself points out the flaws in Jesus' character, and it shows him to be a rather spiteful, nasty fellow ... for example ... 'Think not that I am come to send peace on earth; I came not to send peace, but a sword. For I am come to set a man at variance against his father ... he that

loveth father or mother more than me is not worthy of me.'

This picture of Jesus is far different from the picture of the Messiah that is painted in Isaiah 11, where Isaiah says that the Messiah will bring so much peace that the lion will even be at peace with the calf, and the wolf will be at peace with the lamb.

Thus, the New Testament itself clearly indicates that Jesus and Paul were not the lovely people that they are claimed to be. They were vindictive, hate-breeding liars.[30]

It is almost an insult to the intelligence of anyone reading the present book to point out that not only has Levine taken verses out of context, but he has tried to score points at the expense of Jesus by using arguments which would surely backfire on him if they were used against Orthodox Judaism as well. Jesus' teaching about the virtue of turning the other cheek is to be seen in the context of imitating the love of God, and not allowing the fires of desire for revenge to burn away the capacity for forgiveness, or for sharing with others. He was not condoning evil. And is there nothing compatible in Orthodox Jewish teaching about being ready to 'go the extra mile' with people, to use another phrase of Jesus'? Of course there is!

Jesus' words about bringing a sword come in the context of persecution *against* his followers, not aggression by them. He says to the Jewish people who wish to follow him that others in their homes and society will oppose them, even to the extent of using force against them. And so he asks them to be prepared to have to choose between, on the one hand, giving in to the pressure which will be brought by family, friends, and community leadership, and, on the other hand, persevering in their commitment to him.

This choice is still being faced by Christian people today in different parts of the world. Indeed it is still being faced by Jewish people who come under severe pressure from family and friends when they decide to follow Jesus as the promised Messiah of Israel!

And even here there is an analogy with the situation of Orthodox Judaism. Would Levine agree that there must be something nasty and hateful about Moses too, and indeed about the Torah itself? The situation *often* arises these days that when a secularised Jewish person undergoes a kind of 'conversion' and becomes newly Orthodox, a so-called 'ba'al teshuvah', then this transformation also results in the break-up of the home. In many cases the break is even more upsetting for the parents, or whoever, than if a person becomes interested in Jesus, since the newly Orthodox Jewish person can't eat in their parents' house if it is not 'kosher'. Another typical problem is that newly Orthodox Jews will neither visit, nor be visited by, family or friends on the Sabbath if that entails driving, and therefore breaking the Sabbath. There are several ways like this in which social relationships can be severely strained when one member of a nominally Jewish home becomes observant.

Such tensions and heart-breaks are obviously not the intention of the change of worldview and lifestyle, but they seem to be almost inevitable side-effects. Jesus warned his disciples of the same sort of outcome that would face many of them, and it is that sort of family conflict which Jesus is talking about, as Levine well knows. Levine, and others like him, are fully within their rights to reject the claim that Jesus is the Messiah, but their attempts to ridicule and debase Jesus are a shame in the Jewish community.

No, Jesus' character is there for all to see in the gospels, and I pause once more to encourage Jewish people to read them for themselves.

One other interesting approach has been taken recently by two Jewish scholars of world renown. David Flusser, a professor in the Hebrew University of Jerusalem, in his 1969 book, *Jesus*, and Geza Vermes, whom we have cited already, in his 1973 book, *Jesus the Jew*, both tried to minimize the fact that they themselves were Jewish. This was by no means because they were ashamed of being Jewish. Their intent was to stress that the *Jewish* Jesus is in fact the *only* Jesus there is, the only Jesus that any thoroughly *professional* historical research could ever recover. For them, the faith or heritage of the historian is irrelevant.

In fact Vermes went so far as to give his book the sub-title, 'A Historian's Reading of the Gospels'. He wrote in the opening pages of that work that his intention was

> to discover the authentic, original, historical meaning of the words and events reported in the Gospels.[31]

Clemens Thoma, a non-Jewish Roman Catholic scholar who specializes in the issues of Jewish-Christian relations, accepts this view that certain types of Christian piety have blurred the historical Jesus from our sight and made him difficult to relate to, and so he welcomes any Jewish clarification of the situation.

> Christians have torn Jesus from the soil of Israel. They have de-Judaised, uprooted, alienated, Hellenized, and Europeanized him. The consequences of these manipulations and white-washings are hopeless confusion about the person of Jesus.[32]

So Jewish scholars are able to help, and indeed are helping, to improve historical research into the life of Jesus, though not, of course, without bringing pre-suppositions of their own. Whoever Jesus was, he was more than simply a Jew of his generation. But of course he was also more than some sort of disembodied spirit floating over the hills of Galilee. Jews and Christians therefore are able to help one another to find the real Jesus.

There is a growing confidence in our generation in the historical value of the gospels. We are now dealing with Jewish scholars who regard the gospels as valuable (some would say invaluable) first-century works which, generally speaking, reflect faithfully the actual beliefs, customs and practices of the different Jewish communities of Palestine at that period, and which reflect the actual historical context of Jesus' life. Again it was Joseph Klausner, whom we quoted in an earlier chapter, who broke new ground here in his famous 1922 book, *Jesus of Nazareth*. He said there that there was no justification, in his opinion, for doubt about the historicity of the Gospels.[33]

It is striking, and not a little ironic, to note how Jewish scholars often take liberal Christians to task for not crediting enough historical credibility to the gospels. For example, in 1977 Trude Weiss-Rosmarin was able to state that, as a rule, Jewish students of Jesus gave more credence to the gospels than their Christian counterparts!

> Jewish students of nascent and early Christianity tend to be more 'Gospel true' than modern and contemporary Christian New Testament scholars, who are in agreement that the 'Historical Jesus' is beyond recovery .... [34]

David Flusser of the Hebrew University in Jesusalem opened his book, *Jesus*, with the words:

> The main purpose of this book is to show that it is possible to write the story of Jesus' life.[35]

The words of Max Nordau, the co-founder of the World Zionist Organisation, are especially profound in this regard:

> Jesus is the soul of our soul as he is the flesh of our flesh. Who then could think of excluding him from the people of Israel? St. Peter will remain the only Jew who said of the Son of David: 'I know not the man.'[36]

Of course none of these people believed that Jesus was the Messiah. Their conviction is that Jesus can be, and should be, rooted and grounded in the Judaism of his day. Leo Baeck, the great German statesman of Reform Judaism, made what became an extremely influential remark at the start of this century:

> Most portrayers of the life of Jesus neglect to point out that Jesus is in every characteristic a genuinely Jewish character, that a man like him could have grown only in the soil of Judaism, only there and nowhere else.[37]

In 1913, Rabbi Stephen S.Wise wrote with considerable passion and rhetorical power that Jesus should never have been removed from his only rightful context:

> Jesus should not so much be appreciated by us as assigned to the place in Jewish life and Jewish history which is rightfully his own.[38]

Many Jewish people assume that Jesus does not belong to the Jewish community, in spite of these and other voices urging his reclamation, because he is supposed to have rejected the Jewish religious faith. In 1987, a British rabbi, Dan Cohn-Sherbok, spoke about this in a sermon given in Cambridge. On that occasion, which took place in Great St Mary's Church, he said about Jesus that

His criticism of the religious establishment should not be understood as a rejection of Judaism itself, but as a call to the nation to return to the God of their fathers ... Jesus was anxious to call the people back to the true worship of God ...

Throughout the Gospels Jesus established fellowship with those who were at the margin of society ... he conversed with prostitutes and he welcomed gentiles; he ate with a dishonest tax collector; it is almost certain that he numbered freedom-fighters among his disciples; he allowed women to be among his closest associates.

In other words, Cohn-Sherbok is defending Jesus as a loyal Jewish person. Indeed he is happy to present Jesus as a Jewish person who is worthy of great respect. Jesus is not to be rejected as anti-Jewish. The Jewish community has nothing to fear from Jesus.

Jewish scholars are certainly forcing this issue back onto the agenda, insisting that Jesus cannot be alienated from the Hebrew Bible or the Judaism of his day. If one attempts to de-Judaize Jesus by making him into some sort of all-purpose human being in his relationship to some sort of universal God, rather than by recognizing the indispensable context of his being a *Jewish* worshipper of *Israel's* God, then one commits theological suicide, losing the actual Jesus of history. A non-Jewish Messiah is a contradiction in terms!

Actually this has profound implications for Christians everywhere if they could but see it. As one of my African students said to me recently, 'If Jesus isn't Israel's Messiah, then how can he be anyone else's Christ?' This is a deeply significant and provocative question. The very word, 'Christ', is, of course, simply a Greek version of the Hebrew term, 'Messiah'. Either Jesus is the Messiah or he is not. If he is not the Messiah of Israel, then he cannot be the Messiah, or Christ, of any other people.

But as I have already said, the Jewish scholars whom we have been reading are not motivated by a desire to confirm Christian belief about Jesus as the Messiah of Israel. He is viewed simply as being a great Jewish figure of his time. Zwi Werblowski, one of the leading proponents of Jewish-Christian dialogue in Israel, and a professor at the Hebrew University of Jerusalem, said in 1978 that:

> the activity of Jesus himself and of his disciples is regarded today by most Jewish researchers as being a part, not of the history of Christianity, but that of Judaism.[39]

This is a very significant statement. Christians will take exception to it if it is seen as an attempt to hijack Jesus, as it were, but nonetheless it speaks volumes about the new appeal of Jesus to Jewish people. Equally important is the confident assertion of Pinchas Lapide, an Orthodox Jewish scholar who specializes in Jewish-Christian relations:

> Jesus of Nazareth during his entire life on earth was a pious Jew, and not a Christian ...[40]

And what about the following words of Irving M.

Zeitlin, the professor of Sociology at the University of Toronto:

> Jesus ... was, of course, a Jew, not a Christian ... Jesus the pious Jew fastidiously observed the Law; he celebrated Passover (Mark 14:12ff.), taught in the temple (Mark 14), and wore tsitsit (Mark 6:56) ... [41]

Pinchas Lapide takes to task those who assume that Jesus was not a Jew who kept the Torah. Of course the definition of what constituted keeping the Torah was different then, but Lapide is in no doubt that Jesus kept it in strict accordance with the expectations of the time:

> Jesus was as faithful to the Law as I would hope to be. I even suspect that Jesus was more faithful to the Law than I am—and I am an Orthodox Jew.[42]

This confidence about Jesus' faithfulness to the Torah has gained such currency within the Jewish communities of the West that it is taught almost as a commonplace in some Jewish schools. Here are two typical examples from North American textbooks:

> Jesus was a Jew and taught the best and noblest that was in the Jewish tradition.

> Throughout, we observe that though somewhat of a mystic, Jesus was nonetheless a loyal Jew.[43]

As far as the Jewish community at large is concerned, the most influential Jewish scholar, after Klausner, has been Martin Buber. He presented

Jesus, as we have seen, as his 'brother', and as a uniquely important Jewish figure. But Buber was no 'closet Christian'. Vis-à-vis traditional Judaism, he *elevated* Jesus to the level of great brother, but vis-à-vis traditional Christianity, he *reduced* Jesus to the level of the Jewish people's great brother. It is true that Buber saw Messianic importance in the teaching and life-style of Jesus, but he did not regard Jesus as Israel's Messiah. Jesus was presented by Buber as a model of his famous concept of an 'I-Thou' relationship with God, but this model falls far short of presenting Jesus as the supernatural Son of God of Christian theology.

Most clearly, the theological impasse occurs at the consideration of the resurrection of Jesus. For Jewish scholars (with one very notable exception, as we shall see) this is simply not acceptable as part of the authentic life of Jesus the Jew. In Klausner's programmatic work he comes to the end of his chapter on the death of Jesus with the famous words:

> Here ends the life of Jesus, and here begins the history of Christianity.[44]

David Flusser actually concluded his book on Jesus with the very provocative words:

> And Jesus died.[45]

Schalom Ben-Chorin states unequivocally that in his opinion the Jewish image of Jesus quite naturally comes to a close with the death of Jesus on a cross.

> The Jewish Jesus-image thus recognizes neither
> Christmas with the crib and the star of Bethlehem
> nor Easter with the open grave and the
> resurrection.[46]

The exception to this Jewish consensus is Pinchas Lapide. He asserts that it is quite possible for an Orthodox Jew to accept in principle that God raised Jesus from the dead, since Judaism affirms God as the One who can, in fact, raise the dead back to life. There are even prayers to this effect in the regular synagogue liturgy.

However, Lapide insists, this would not of itself constitute proof that Jesus was the Messiah, let alone that he was divine, since the Bible itself relates other accounts of mere mortals being brought back to life by the power of God. But this approach of Lapide's has not won support within the Jewish community. The religious and community leaders have judged it to be too risky to let the Jewish population think positively about the resurrection of Jesus.[47]

While respecting that decision, it is nonetheless hoped that enough has been presented in this book so far to show that Jewish people will not be struck down by lightning if they listen to Jesus for themselves. The very experience of reading the gospels is an eye-opening one for many. The gospels even read like a Jewish account of a Jewish person's life. Listen to these words from a Jerusalem scholar who was working in the late 1950s on a translation of the gospel of Mark into Hebrew for the growing number of Israeli, Hebrew-speaking congregations of Jewish believers in Jesus:

Rather to my surprise the preliminary study of the Greek text of Mark turned up the conclusion that the Greek word order and idiom was more like Hebrew than literary Greek. This gave me the frightening feeling that I was as much in the process of 'restoring' an original Hebrew work as in that of creating a new one.[48]

Is it unreasonable, then, to want to encourage Jewish people to discover the gospels for themselves? It will come as a revelation to them to realise just how Jewish the gospels are.

9

The Coming Messiah

The great issue between Jews and Christians today, at least in most quarters, is no longer whether or not Jesus was a bona fide Jewish teacher; nor is there any bitter controversy as to whether or not he played a prophetic role in the life of Israel at the end of the second temple period, though some will want to deny him the prophetic mantle. No, attention has been focused elsewhere in our generation.

Clearly the largest single difference between Jews and Christians on the issue of the identity of Jesus is found in the answer to the question as to whether he is not only a great Jewish teacher of his time, and possibly also a prophetic figure of some considerable stature, but also the promised Messiah of Israel. We have come full circle to the opening generations of the Common Era.

The previous chapters of this book will have made it clear that the Jewish world as a whole does not accept that Jesus is the Messiah. However, the reason for this has much more to do with the Jewish community's terrible suffering at the hands of the Church than it has to do with any careful and honest assessment of the person, teaching and work of Jesus himself. Having said that, of course, no one could fail to sympathise with the Jewish attitude which says that you can perhaps best judge a person by his or her followers.

On the other hand, Jesus is still calling to Jewish people to let him speak to them face to face, as it were. The fact that there is strong pressure from the Jewish community against this should not be allowed to prevent an open attitude to Jesus. In fact several Jewish scholars, as we have seen, have already begun to challenge this anti-Jesus pressure.

But most astonishingly, comes the development which I will now mention. Each of the past three decades has produced a startling statement from a significant Jewish thinker, perhaps helping to provide a liberation, a permission, if you like, for the present generation to really think for themselves.

> …it might well be that He who comes at the end of time, He who has been alike the expectation of the synagogue and the church, will bear one and the same countenance.[49]

> It seems to me that very few Jews would protest if the Messiah, when he comes, should turn out to be the Jew Jesus.[50]

> I am happily prepared to wait until the coming one comes and if he should show himself to be Jesus of

Nazareth, I cannot imagine that even a single Jew who believes in God would have the least thing against that.[51]

These statements are very suggestive. Of course they are not at all typical of sentiments within the Jewish community, though that does not detract from their significance. But before going any further on this matter, it is surely time to do some introducing of the actual teachings and actions of Jesus, in order to provide clues to what will be found when the gospels are opened for themselves.

What kind of person is Jesus? He is a 'people person', as we like to say nowadays. All sorts of people wanted to spend time with him, as we read in the gospels, and this is just as true today.

In the gospels we see him in the company of street people (prostitutes among them), everyday workers (like fishermen and tradesmen), religious leaders of different persuasions, women of all sorts (whom Jesus spent time with for their own sake), and political extremists (as the zealots were). He was not alwayscomfortable to be around, but his spiritual and moral challenges to people struck home very deeply, attracting those who were sincerely searching for a right relationship with God. It is clear from the gospels that Jesus had a real concern and respect for women. What is also evident is his love for children, and for the disadvantaged of all types.

Several times we are told of his strong compassion for people in pain and difficult circumstances. Much of the account preserved for us tells us about his commitment to healing people. Jesus went so far as to heal the sick on the Sabbath. There was great pressure from the religious establishment to postpone until another day any healing which could be put off without danger to the suffering person. But Jesus countered by insisting that there could not be any better day *than* the Sabbath on which to heal the sick, thus celebrating God's good creation and re-creation of life!

Another characteristic of Jesus about which we are often told is his authority as a teacher, and as a living model, of the life and love of God. This is not to denigrate in any way the wisdom or piety of any others, but it is the recognition that Jesus had (and has) an authority which was, quite simply, amazing. Jesus' words had power, and this in two senses. On the one hand people knew that he spoke the truth when he questioned them or answered their questions, whether they liked the truth or not; and on the other hand he was able to do everything which he said he could do, in terms of healing people and performing miracles.

Central to Jesus' teaching was the reality and the imminence of the Kingdom of God, or, as he would have called it, the Kingdom of Heaven. This is not a geographical term, of course, but means the active rule of God in the world. When God is in charge of your life then you are part of the Kingdom of God. Also characteristic was Jesus' stress on the truth that God is our Father, concerned about us, loving us, longing for a real relationship with us. He spoke to

God calling Him 'Abba', a term of warm affection, loving respect, and trusting surrender.

Using the texts of Deuteronomy 6:5 ('love the Lord your God with all your heart, soul, and strength') and Leviticus 19:18 ('love your neighbour as yourself'), Jesus taught that life was about loving God with all of one's being, and then also loving every other person whom God had created in His image.

This all adds up to an incredibly attractive and powerful person who made an irreversible difference to all those who came into real contact with him. Jesus was killed on an execution stake by the Roman authorities (though his death was not mourned by certain Jewish leaders). The gospels then go on to tell us that God raised him back to life, and that he shared the power of his resurrection with his followers. Countless followers of Jesus from that time till now, numbering many Jewish believers among them, testify that he is as alive today as he ever was. He still makes that real difference to the people, Jewish and non-Jewish, who come into real contact with him.

I am conscious that although we have looked at a good number of texts from the gospels in this book, and done a fair amount of analysis and evaluation, the great bulk of the material has been in the nature of discussions about Jesus. So, it is now time to let the gospels speak for themselves. The next chapter will take the form of an extensive series of quotations from the gospel of Matthew, focusing on the words and actions of Jesus himself. They are, in a real sense, the core and the goal of this book.

10

Jesus Ben Joseph—The Messiah

All the following readings are taken from the gospel of Matthew, the opening book in the New Testament. They are intended to be an indication of what awaits the reader who opens up the gospels for him/herself.

There are many translations available, and the one chosen here is one which was made by an Israeli Messianic Jewish scholar, David Stern, in 1989.[52]

Significant Jewish terms are left untranslated by Stern, as will be obvious in this selection of passages.

It should be especially noted that he uses the Hebrew form of Jesus' name, Yeshua, discussed in a former chapter.

Some words of Jesus.

Seeing the crowds, Yeshua walked up the hill. After he sat down, his talmidim came to him, and he began to speak. This is what he taught them:

'How blessed are the poor in spirit!
for the Kingdom of Heaven is theirs.
How blessed are those who mourn!
for they will be comforted.
How blessed are the meek!
for they will inherit the Land.
How blessed are those who hunger
and thirst for righteousness!
for they will be filled.
How blessed are those who show mercy!
for they will be shown mercy.
How blessed are the pure in heart!
for they will see God.
How blessed are those who make peace!
for they will be called sons of God.
How blessed are those who are persecuted
because they pursue righteousness!
for the Kingdom of Heaven is theirs.'
(Matt.5:1-10)

'You are salt for the Land. But if salt becomes taste-less, how can it be made salty again? It is no longer good for anything except being thrown out for people to trample on. You are light for the world. A town built on a hill cannot be hidden. Likewise, when people light a lamp, they don't cover it with a bowl, but put it on a lampstand, so that it shines for everyone in the house. In the same way, let your light shine before people, so that they may see the good things you do and praise your Father in heaven.' *(Matt.5:13-16)*

'Don't think that I have come to abolish the Torah or
the Prophets. I have come not to abolish but to
complete. Yes indeed! I tell you that until
heaven and earth pass away, not so much as a
yud or a stroke will pass from the Torah—not
until everything that must happen has happened.' *(Matt.5:17f.)*

'Be careful not to parade your acts of tzedakah in
front of people in order to be seen by them! If
you do, you have no reward from your Father in
heaven. So, when you do tzedakah, don't
announce it with trumpets to win people's
praise, like the hypocrites … Yes! I tell you,
they have their reward already! But you, when
you do tzedakah, don't even let your left hand
know what your right hand is doing. Then your
tzedakah will be in secret; and your Father, who
sees what you do in secret, will reward you.'
(Matt.6:1-4)

'When you pray, don't be like the hypocrites … Yes!
I tell you, they have their reward already! But
you, when you pray, go into your room, close
the door, and pray to your Father in secret.
Your Father, who sees what is done in secret,
will reward you. And when you pray, don't
babble on and on like the pagans, who think
God will hear them better if they talk a lot.
Don't be like them, because your Father knows
what you need before you ask him. You, therefore, pray like this:

Our Father in heaven!
>May your Name be kept holy.
>May your Kingdom come, your will be done on
>earth as in heaven.
>Give us the food we need today.
>Forgive us what we have done wrong,
>as we too have forgiven those who have
>wronged us.
>And do not lead us into hard testing,
>but keep us safe from the Evil One.
>For kingship, power and glory are yours for-
>ever.
>Amen.' *(Matt.6:5-13)*

'Keep asking, and it will be given to you; keep seeking, and you will find; keep knocking, and the
door will be opened to you. For everyone who
keeps asking receives; he who keeps seeking
finds; and to him who keeps knocking, the door
will be opened.' *(Matt.7:7f.)*

'My Father has handed over everything to me.
Indeed, no one fully knows the Son except the
Father, and no one fully knows the Father
except the Son and those to whom the Son
wishes to reveal him. Come to me, all of you
who are struggling and burdened, and I will
give you rest. Take my yoke upon you and learn
from me, because I am gentle and humble in
heart, and you will find rest for your souls. For
my yoke is easy , and my burden is light.'
(Matt.11:27-30)

'The Kingdom of Heaven is like a treasure hidden in a field. A man found it, hid it again, then in great joy went and sold everything he owned, and bought that field.' *(Matt.13:44)*

At that moment the talmidim came to Yeshua and asked, 'Who is the greatest in the Kingdom of Heaven?' He called a child to him, stood him among them, and said, 'Yes! I tell you that unless you change and become like little children, you won't even enter the Kingdom of Heaven! So the greatest in the Kingdom is whoever makes himself as humble as this child.' *(Matt.18:1-4)*

When the crowds heard how he taught, they were astounded; but when the P'rushim learned that he had silenced the Tz'dukim ... one of them who was a Torah expert asked a sh'eilah ... 'Rabbi, which of the mitzvot in the Torah is the most important?' He told him, 'You are to love Adonai your God with all your heart and with all your soul and with all your strength. This is the greatest and most important mitzvah. And a second is similar to it, You are to love your neighbour as yourself. All of the Torah and the Prophets are dependent on these two mitzvot.' *(Matt.22:33-40)*

Some acts of Jesus.

After Yeshua had come down from the hill, large
crowds followed him. Then a man afflicted with
a repulsive skin disease came, kneeled down in
front of him and said, 'Sir, if you are willing,
you can make me clean.' Yeshua reached out
his hand, touched him and said, 'I am willing!
Be cleansed!' And at once he was cleansed from
his skin disease. Then Yeshua said to him, 'See
that you tell no one; but as a testimony to the
people, go and let the cohen examine you, and
offer the sacrifice that Moshe commanded.'
(Matt.8:1-4)

While he was talking, an official came in, kneeled
down in front of him and said, 'My daughter
has just died. But if you come and lay your
hand on her, she will live.' Yeshua, with his
talmidim, got up and followed him. A woman
who had had a haemorrhage for twelve years
approached him from behind and touched the
tzitzit on his robe. For she said to herself, 'If I
can only touch his robe, I will be healed.' Yeshua turned, saw her and said, 'Courage, daughter! Your trust has healed you.' And she was
instantly healed.

When Yeshua arrived at the official's house and
saw the flute-players, and the crowd in an
uproar, he said, 'Everybody out! The girl isn't
dead, she's only sleeping!' And they jeered at
him. But after the people had been put outside,

140

he entered and took hold of the girl's hand, and she got up. News of this spread through all that region. *(Matt.9:18-26)*

As evening approached, the talmidim came to him and said, 'This is a remote place and it's getting late. Send the crowds away, so that they can go and buy food for themselves in the villages.' But Yeshua replied, 'They don't need to go away. Give them something to eat, yourselves!' 'All we have with us,' they said, 'is five loaves of bread and two fish.' He said, 'Bring them here to me.' After instructing the crowds to sit down on the grass, he took the five loaves and the two fish and, looking up toward heaven, made a b'rakhah. Then he broke the loaves and gave them to the talmidim, who gave them to the crowds. They all ate as much as they wanted, and they took up twelve baskets full of the pieces left over. Those eating numbered about five thousand men, plus women and children. *(Matt.14:15-21)*

The authority of Jesus.

Some people brought him a paralyzed man lying on a mattress. When Yeshua saw their trust, he said to the paralyzed man, 'Courage, son! Your sins are forgiven.' On seeing this, some of the Torah-teachers said among themselves, 'This man is blaspheming!' Yeshua, knowing what

they were thinking, said, 'Why are you enter-
taining evil thoughts in your hearts? Tell me,
which is easier to say—Your sins are forgiven
or Get up and walk? But look! I will prove to
you that the Son of Man has authority on earth
to forgive sins.' He then said to the paralyzed
man, 'Get up, pick up your mattress, and go
home!' And the man got up and went home.
(Matt.9:2-7)

Jesus' death and resurrection.

The governor's soldiers took Yeshua into the head-
quarters building, and the whole battalion
gathered around him. They stripped off his
clothes and put on him a scarlet robe, wove
thorn branches into a crown and put it on his
head, and put a stick in his right hand. Then
they kneeled down in front of him and made fun
of him: 'Hail to the King of the Jews!' They spat
on him and used the stick to beat him about the
head. When they had finished ridiculing him,
they took off the robe, put his own clothes back
on him and led him away to be nailed to the
execution-stake ... After they had nailed him to
the stake, they divided his clothes among them
by throwing dice. Then they sat down to keep
watch over him there ... Yeshua ... yielded up
his spirit...

After Shabbat, toward dawn on Sunday, Miryam
of Magdala and the other Miryam went to see

the grave. Suddenly there was a violent earth-quake, for an angel of Adonai came down from heaven, rolled away the stone and sat on it. His appearance was like lightning, and his clothes were as white as snow. The guards were so terrified at him that they trembled and became like dead men. But the angel said to the women, 'Don't be afraid. I know you are looking for Yeshua, who was executed at the stake. He is not here, because he has been raised—just as he said! Come and look at the place where he lay. Then go quickly and tell the talmidim, He has been raised from the dead, and now he is going to the Galil ahead of you. You will see him there …

So the eleven talmidim went to the hill in the Galil where Yeshua had told them to go. When they saw him, they prostrated themselves before him; but some hesitated. Yeshua came and talked with them. He said, 'All authority in heaven and on earth has been given to me. Therefore, go and make people from all nations into talmidim, immersing them into the reality of the Father, the Son and the Ruach Ha-Kodesh, and teaching them to obey everything that I have commanded you. And remember! I will be with you always, yes, even until the end of the age.' *(Matt.27:27-31, 35f., 50; 28:1-7, 16-20)*

I hope that something of the person of Jesus comes through in this selection of passages. Nothing compensates for reading the whole gospel, of course.

Postscript

The past three decades in particular have seen the growth of two quite different movements of Jewish rediscovery of the Jewishness of Jesus. Both of them are remarkable. On the one hand there has been the rapid expansion of scholarly interest in Jesus the Jew from Galilee. Much of the present book has been looking at this very issue. Jesus is being 'de-mythologised' and restored, as these scholars would have it, to his rightful status as a faithful Jewish teacher of his time and place. Tremendous insights into the social and religious world of Jesus have emerged from this work, and Christians everywhere should be grateful for it.

But on the other hand there has been the equally rapid growth of what is generally known as the Messianic Jewish movement. This refers to those Jewish people who have come to believe that Jesus was not only Jewish, but in fact the Messiah. There has always been a part of the Jewish community which believed in Jesus, even though these people often had to keep their faith a secret from others, and sometimes the numbers in certain regions were quite large. But there can be no doubting the size and momentum of this contemporary movement.

Understandably, perhaps, this very conviction of the Messiahship of Jesus by Messianic Jews has been a significant factor in persuading some Jewish leaders to discourage Jewish people from taking advantage of the new openness towards Jesus which is now possible for them. At the same time, other Jewish leaders are aggressively advocating that Jews and Christians alike turn their backs once and for all on the orthodox Christian understanding of Jesus, and interpret him as simply a great Jewish man.

There are three myths concerning any serious study of the life and teaching of Jesus which still have power in the Jewish community today:

a) Jesus is not really Jewish, and so to study his life is not acceptable Jewish research.

b) Jewish scholarship wants nothing to do with Jesus in any positive sense, and so to want to study his life will put you on the margins of scholarship.

c) Jewish people will somehow come to harm if they read a gospel account of Jesus for themselves.

I hope that any Jewish person reading this book will realise that none of these myths is true. I also hope that he or she will go on to consider the great adventure of encountering Jesus ben Joseph for her or himself.

Notes

1. Martin Buber: *Two Types of Faith* (N.Y., Harper & Row, 1961), p.12.
2. Claude Montefiore, in the *Jewish Quarterly Review*, 1894, page 381. Sixteen years later he was still of the same opinion, and said in his 1910 work, *Some Elements of the Religious Teaching of Jesus*, that 'God's nearness was felt by Jesus directly, with a vivid intensity unsurpassed by any man.' (p.88)
3. Joseph Klausner: *Jesus of Nazareth: His Life, Times, and Teaching* (N.Y., Macmillan, 1925), p.414.
4. Op.cit., pp.12f.
5. Geza Vermes: *Jesus the Jew*, (London, Collins, 1973), p.224.
6. Pinchas Lapide and Peter Stuhlmacher: *Paul, Rabbi and Apostle* (ET, Minneapolis, Augsburg Publishing House, 1984, from a 1981 original), p.31.

7. Albert Schweitzer: *The Quest of the Historical Jesus* (3rd edition, London, Adam & Charles Black, 1954), p.397.

8. Bernard J.Lee: *The Galilean Jewishness of Jesus* (N.Y., Paulist Press, 1988), p.57.

9. Naim Stifan Ateek: *Justice, And Only Justice. A Palestinian Theology of Liberation* (N.Y., Orbis Books, 1989), p.113. The second quotation comes from an address by Hanan Ashrawi, the spokeswoman for the Palestinian delegation to the Middle East Peace Conference in Madrid, 1991.

10. Geza Vermes: *Jesus the Jew*, op.cit., pp.69, 223.

11. Op.cit., p.224.

12. Hyam Maccoby: *Revolution In Judaea. Jesus And The Jewish Resistance* (London, Orbach and Chambers, 1973), pp.123, 131f.

13. Harvey Falk: *Jesus the Pharisee. A New Look at the Jewishness of Jesus* (Mahwah, N.J., Paulist Press, 1985), p.158.

14. Ibid.

15. Op.cit., pp.30, 19.

16. Julius Wellhausen: *Einleitung in die drei ersten Evangelien* (Berlin, Reimar,1905), p.113. His actual words were: 'Jesus war kein Christ sondern Jude.'

17. *The Mishnah:* Yebamot 4:13.

18. *The Babylonian Talmud:* Sanhedrin 67a.

19. *The Babylonian Talmud:* Sanhedrin 43a.

20. *The Babylonian Talmud:* Sanhedrin 106a.

21. *The Babylonian Talmud:* Sanhedrin 43a.

22. Solomon Schechter: 'Genizah Specimens', *Jewish Quarterly Review*, vol.10, pp.65-67.

23. Hugh J.Schonfield: *According to the Hebrews* (London, Duckworth, 1937), p.37.

24. Op.cit., pp.39-41.

25. Quoted in David Novak: *Jewish-Christian Dialogue. A Jewish Justification* (Oxford, OUP, 1989), p.78.

26. Op.cit., p.84.

27. Emma Felsenthal: *Bernard Felsenthal, Teacher in Israel* (N.Y., 1924), p.265.

28. This is quoted in Novak, op.cit., p.80.

29. Isaac Mayer Wise: *The Martyrdom of Jesus of Nazareth* (N.Y., 1888), p.132.

30. Samuel Levine: *You Take Jesus, I'll Take God* (Los Angeles, Hamoroh Press, 1980), pp.82, 83, 90, 91.

31. Op.cit., p.16. He closes the book by summing it up as a 'first step in what seems to be the direction of the real man'. (p.224).

32. Clemens Thoma: *A Christian Theology of Judaism* (N.Y., Paulist Press, 1980), p.107.

33. Op.cit. pp.126f.

34. Trude Weiss-Rosmarin (ed.): *Jewish Expressions on Jesus. An Anthology* (N.Y., Ktav, 1977), p.ix.

35. David Flusser: *Jesus* (N.Y., Herder and Herder, 1969), p.7.

36. Schalom Ben-Chorin quotes these words very favourably in his book, *Bruder Jesu: Der Nazarener in judischer Sicht* (Munich, List, 1967), p.11.

37. As quoted by Schalom Ben-Chorin in, 'The Image of Jesus in Modern Judaism', *Journal of Ecumenical Studies*, vol.11, no.3, Summer 1974, p.408.

38. Wise wrote in the June 7th edition of the magazine, *The Outlook*.

39. 'Jesus devant la Pensé Juive Contemporaine', in *Les Grandes Religions*, 1978, p.36.

40. Lapide and Stuhlmacher, *Paul, Rabbi and Apostle*, op.cit., p.50.

41. Irving M.Zeitlin: *Jesus and the Judaism of His Time* (N.Y., Polity Press, 1988), pp.48, 52, 63.

42. Pinchas Lapide and Hans Kung: 'Is Jesus a Bond or Barrier? A Jewish-Christian Dialogue', *Journal of Ecumenical Studies* 14, Summer 1977, p.473. See also David Flusser, op. cit., p.10.

43. William B.Silverman: *Judaism and Christianity: What We Believe*, 1968, p.93; Milton G.Miller: *Our Religion and Our Neighbours*, rev.ed., 1971, p.59.

44. Op.cit., p.355.

45. Flusser: *Jesus*, op.cit., p.132.

46. Art.cit., p.427.

47. Pinchas Lapide: *The Resurrection Of Jesus* (London, SPCK, 1984).

48. Robert L.Lindsey: *A Hebrew Translation Of The Gospel Of Mark* (Jerusalem, Dugith Publishers, 1973), pp.9f. Some of the implications of that discovery are taken up by David Bivin in his book, *Understanding the difficult words of Jesus* (Arcadia, CA, Makor Foundation, 1983).

49. Hans Joachim Schoeps: *Paul—The Theology of the Apostle in the Light of Jewish Religious History* (Philadelphia, Westminster Press, 1961), p.258.

50. David Flusser: 'Jezus als vraag aan joden en christenen', in *Concilium*, 11, 8, 1974, p.133.

51. Pinchas Lapide and Jurgen Moltmann: *Jewish Monotheism and Christian Trinitarian Doctrine* (Philadelphia, Fortress Press, 1981), p.79.
52. David H.Stern: *Jewish New Testament* (Jerusalem, Jerusalem New Testament Publications, 1989).

If you would like to know more about Jesus, just tick the appropriate box(es):

☐ Please send me a New Testament in Hebrew/English
☐ Please send me free literature
☐ I would like to talk to someone who can tell me more.

Name (Dr/Mr/Mrs/Miss/Ms)

Address

Postcode

Please send to:

Dr Walter Riggans
All Nations Christian College
Easneye
Ware
Herts SG12 8LX

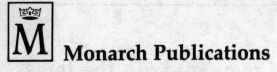

Monarch Publications
Books of Substance

All Monarch books can be purchased from your local Christian or general bookshop. In case of difficulty they may be ordered from the publisher:

> Monarch Publications
> PO Box 163
> Tunbridge Wells
> Kent
> TN3 0NZ

Please enclose a cheque payable to Monarch Publications for the cover price plus: 60p for the first book ordered plus 40p per copy for each additional book, to a maximum charge of £3.00 to cover postage and packing (UK and Republic of Ireland only).

Overseas customers please order from:

Christian Marketing PTY Ltd
PO Box 154
North Geelong
Victoria 3215
Australia

Omega Distributors Ltd
69 Great South Road
Remuera
Auckland
New Zealand

Struik Christian Books
80 McKenzie Street Gardens
Cape Town 8001
South Africa

Kingsway USA Inc
4717 Hunter's Crossing
  Drive
Old Hickory
TN 37138
USA

Christian Marketing
Canada
Box 7000
Niagara-on-the-Lake
Ontario LOS 1JO
Canada

The Covenant with the Jews

Walter Riggans

God once made a covenant with the Jews. Has he
abandoned his promises—in favour of the Church? The
Church has a shameful history of anti-semitism: is this
because Christians think of themselves as the inheritors
of God's favour? Are the Messianic Jesws, who remain
culturally Jewish but accept Jesus as their Messiah, the
key to the situation?

In answering these questions, the author motivtes us to
explore our heritage more deeply. 'Evangelicals must
learn to appreciate the insights of Judaism,' suggests
Walter Riggans. 'They need to come to the point of
genuine repentance for Christian anti-semitism. At the
same time we must never lose sight of the fact that Jesus
is Israel's one and only Messiah, and that our biblical
mandate is to share this truth with the Jewish people.'

The Rev Dr Walter Riggans lived in Israel for nine years,
and spent three of them as Director of the Church's
Ministry among the Jews in Tel Aviv. He is now a tutor at
All Nations Christian College in Ware, Hertfordshire.

ISBN 1 85424 188 5

Monarch
Publications

Messianic Jews:
The Search For Identity

John Fieldsend

One of the most significant phenomena of the church today must be the growth of the Messianic Jewish movement—Jewish people who have come to realise that Jesus of Nazareth really is the Messiah of Israel and the Son of God.

Of course there have always been such Jewish people in our churches, but today we are seeing the commitment of many of them to develop their own congregations and lifestyle, based on their Jewishness as well as their New Testament faith. Is this dangerous, or exciting and appropriate?

In this important and very readable book John Fieldsend, himself a British Messianic Jewish leader, helps us to explore the beliefs and practices of Messianic Jews today. He covers the nature of contemporary Judaism, the objections for both Jews and Christians, the chief characteristics of Messianic Judaism, and the part it can play in shaping the future development of the Body of Christ.

Co-published with Olive Press.

ISBN 1 85424 228 8

Monarch
Publications